CAMBRIDGE SURVEYS OF ECONOMIC LITERATURE

MICROFOUNDATIONS

THE COMPATIBILITY OF MICROECONOMICS
AND MACROECONOMICS

CAMBRIDGE SURVEYS OF ECONOMIC LITERATURE

The literature of economics is expanding rapidly and many subjects have changed out of recognition within the space of a few years. Perceiving the state of knowledge in fast-developing subjects is difficult for students and time-consuming for professional economists. This series of books is intended to help with this problem. Each book will be quite brief, giving a clear structure to and balanced overview of the topic and written at a level intelligible to the senior undergraduate. They will therefore be useful for teaching, but will also provide a mature yet compact presentation of the subject for the economist wishing to update his knowledge outside his own specialism.

Microfoundations

THE COMPATIBILITY OF
MICROECONOMICS AND MACROECONOMICS

E. ROY WEINTRAUB

Professor of Economics, Duke University

CAMBRIDGE UNIVERSITY PRESS

CAMBRIDGE

LONDON · NEW YORK · MELBOURNE

Published by the Syndics of the Cambridge University Press
The Pitt Building, Trumpington Street, Cambridge CB2 1RP
Bentley House, 200 Euston Road, London NW1 2DB
32 East 57th Street, New York, NY 10022, USA
296 Beaconsfield Parade, Middle Park, Melbourne 3206, Australia

First published 1979

Printed in the United States of America
Photoset by The Pitman Press, Bath, England
Printed and bound by Vail-Ballou Press, Inc., Binghamton, New York

Library of Congress Cataloguing in Publication Data

Weintraub, E Roy.
Microfoundations: the compatibility of microeconomics and macroeconomics.

(Cambridge surveys of economic literature)
Bibliography: p.
Includes index.
1. Microeconomics. 2. Macroeconomics. 3. Equilibrium (Economics).
4. Economics—Mathematical models.
I. Title.
HB71.W397   330.1   78-16551
ISBN 0 521 22305 9 hardcovers
ISBN 0 521 29445 2 paperback

CONTENTS

PREFACE

The relationship between microeconomic theory and macro-economic theory has been stormy. The subject has been ignored, discovered, settled and ignored again. The literature is replete with polemics, calls to action, and technical preciousness which obscure the central ideas. Consequently this book is a survey organized around the question "Are the concerns and models of micro-economic theory logically consistent with the concerns and models of macroeconomic theory?"

My biases should be recognized. I consider economic theory to be a scientific discipline. I believe that our knowledge is more secure if our insights can be developed in terms of formal models. I believe that progress occurs in terms of sequences of models which have assumptions that are clear and conclusions that are falsifiable either by empirical tests or by tests of congruence with other theoretical constructs.

Having been trained as a mathematician, I am less impressed with mathematical virtuosity than some economists. However that same training leaves me suspicious of analyses that begin with an ideologically "correct" view and end with conclusions which support that view.

My own approach to microfoundations issues can be summed up by Axel Leijonhufvud's observation, noted in Chapter 5, that

> Mathematical general equilibrium theorists have at their

command an impressive array of proven techniques for modelling systems that "always work well." Keynesian economists have experience with modelling systems that "never work." But, as yet, no one has the recipe for modelling systems that function pretty well most of the time but sometimes work very badly to coordinate economic activities. And the analytical devices and routines of neo-Walrasian general equilibrium theory and Keynesian theory will not "mix" [Leijonhufvud, 1976, p. 103].

The degree of mathematical sophistication required by the reader is not extensive. Professional economists, first-year graduate students, or third-year U.K. honors students all should be able to follow the exposition.

Several individuals have given me comments and advice on this project from its inception as a *Journal of Economic Literature* article to its current form as an extended survey. Neil de Marchi, Warren Weber, Michael Rothschild, Paul Davidson, H. Gregg Lewis, and John Weymark represent what, to me, is good about the economics profession: it is concerned that ideas be taken seriously. Mark Perlman, first sponsor of this project, has been the very model of a modern journal editor. His support and encouragement have been of inestimable value.

This book is dedicated to Garth, who found several pages of the manuscript quite tasty, but rather dry.

E. Roy Weintraub
Durham, North Carolina
October, 1977

Part I

Introduction

It is always difficult to appraise current research in an area, especially in a technical area, for a non-specialist. Recent work on problems associated with the microfoundations of macroeconomics present severe difficulties since the literature is intrinsically integrative, albeit abstract. The particular set of abstractions, or models, have their roots in the separate concerns of micro-economists, general equilibrium theorists, macroeconomists, and monetary theorists and as such cannot be fully appreciated without a sense of how these areas have developed and interacted up to the present time.

In a discipline like economics, where progress can be identified with sequences of models each successively better suited to the current issues, but each always developing from a predecessor, an understanding of what is "modern" requires too an understanding of what is no longer "modern."

The basic structure of Part I represents what must be an imperfect attempt to trace the development and interlocking nature of two scientific research programs (in the sense of Lakatos), macroeconomic theory and (general equilibrium) neo-Walrasian theory. Since much that is currently being done in the various microfoundations literatures can be identified as the symbiosis of these two programs, their separate developments should be part of the mental baggage of modern economists.

In Chapter 1, then, a case is built that the set of problems being considered ramifies in a multitude of ways into the daily thinking of professional economists who believe themselves quite free of, and apart from, the arcane concerns of mathematical economists.

Chapter 2 examines the development of what is termed "neo-Walrasianism." Modern general equilibrium theory began in the 1930s and reached fruition by around 1960. Textbooks treat these issues, however, as though they occurred all at once, and all of a piece. In fact, they did not, and it is this which gave substance to the Keynesian revolution.

In Chapter 3 Keynes' system is examined, for it gave macroeconomics its new birth. Following others we shall identify at least two Keyneses, neither of whom is well established in the textbook versions of macroeconomics.

Chapter 4 examines the synthesis between neo-Walrasian methods and "Keynesian" approaches, and suggests how the modern Keynesian analysis was shaped by the strength of the neo-Walrasian research program.

Finally, in Chapter 5, the "caution" flags go up and the deviant voices of Clower and Leijonhufvud are heard to exclaim, *a propos* the misnamed "neoclassical synthesis," "But the emperor has no clothes!" Their attempts to redress the issues will appear as a motif thoughout Part II.

1

Points of entry

To many economists there is a clear interrelationship between microeconomics and macroeconomics. If asked by a student to explain how micro profit maximization constrains a macromodel, the economist might describe aggregate supply as an aggregate production function, and the demand for labor as a derived demand which, under competitive profit maximization conditions, can be set equal to the real wage rate. If asked about the relation between the theory of consumer behaviour and the theory of the consumption function, the economist may produce a sophisticated utility maximization framework. Constraints involve income and wealth such that, for given tastes and prices, real consumption demand depends on real disposable income appropriately defined.

The microeconomic foundations of the aggregate demand for money can be similarly located in choice-theoretic portfolio analysis or inventory analysis. The demand for capital goods may be studied as part of firms' desires to maximize discounted net worth.

If the student wished to press further, there is a set of questions which could be developed at a higher level of abstraction. "How," it might be asked, "is it possible to generate labor market excess supply in equilibrium, when in microeconomics we were taught that excess demand was zero in equilibrium?" The standard answers here probably vary with the training of the instructor, but most economists would describe the difference between partial equilibrium analysis and general equilibrium theory, and suggest that in a multi-market framework, disturbances or structural rigidities in one market may induce disequilibrium in another market. Thus perhaps a liquidity trap in the money market or an insensitivity of investment to the interest rate could produce the labor market unemployment. The various answers which would be given to the question would likely share the presumption that indeed unemployment *is* something whose existence needs to be explained. It is not often that microeconomic reasoning works away from equilibrium positions.

In a first pass at issues of the microfoundations of macro-economics, roughly at the level of an intermediate theory course, economists teach (pretend to believe?) that micro-economic theory is wholly reconcilable with macroeconomics. At the graduate level, however, there is a professional's desire for more rigorous modelling, and consequently classes pay explicit attention to the macroeconomic implications of a well-specified general equilibrium system. An instructor might lecture on a sequence of general equilibrium models, each of increasing complexity. The students would come to understand how the assumptions of individual and firm behavior, and the distribution mechanisms which complete the circular flow, generate competitive equilibria. Optimality propositions, and comparative static results, would often be presented; differences in assumptions made about "kinds" of money and other assets would entail different final outcomes. After a discussion of the aggregation problem, individuals and firms would be aggregated to a several market model (usually goods, money, bonds, and labor) and the macroeconomic content could be traced directly to the micro-economic specifications.

There would be some discussion of the logical difficulties of this program with the micro-treatment of expectations, the weakness of the institutional description, aggregation problems, and the absence of monopoly elements. Other technical problems, like establishing existence, uniqueness, and stability of the micro-economic equilibrium, may be slighted as the argument speeds toward the induced macro-model and its properties. Yet even in this more sophisticated pedagogy, there is an implicit affirmation of logical compatibility between what is generally accepted as standard microeconomics and what is generally accepted as standard macroeconomics.

Without *ad hominem* detours into the "pop" sociology of economics, it may still be worth while, in an informal manner befiting an introductory chapter, to consider why a belief in micro–macro consistency is shared by many economists.

For those economists who are applied microeconomists, their training involved the accumulation of a set of tools and approaches. Concepts of scarcity, choice, costs and benefits, and efficient outcomes are the content of standard analysis, and the microeconomic theory from which these concepts are derived is the central core of neoclassical theory. This theory has been, and continues to be, successful both in predicting novel facts and in structuring questions about economic life. It makes generating predictions tractable.

Consequently any question about microfoundations of macroeconomics which could conceivably vitiate neoclassical analysis would be strongly resisted. The benefits to be gained from the ability to handle anomalies might not at present compensate our science for the immense cost of not being able to answer questions which are handled in a now routine fashion. Further, the anomaly would have to be both generally recognized and perceived to be serious to even consider redirecting microeconomics. But even the few economists who argue that current microeconomics *does not generate* macroeconomics have been extremely shy in their attempts to convince their colleagues of the seriousness of their concerns.

For macroeconomists, the question is somewhat more pressing since accepting the current micro–macro linkages severely constrains macroeconomic modelling. There appears to be only one legitimate macroeconomic mode of discourse when conformability with general equilibrium theory is presupposed. Alternative macroeconomic theories, like those of the Post-Keynesians, fall outside the pale of legitimate discourse. Monetarist–fiscalist debates must be carried on in an intellectual framework that practically ensures the audience that the debate will be reduced to one of "both sides are partially correct; it's all a matter of degree." Giving up the underpinnings of macroeconomic theory would grant hegemony to disparate interpretations of inflation, unemployment, growth, and distribution. Neo-Marxians and monetarists would argue about matters of practical policy with no common ground or shared presuppositions.

Finally, from the viewpoint of historians of economics and those who believe in progress and continuity within a discipline, arguments which suggest that microeconomics and macroeconomics are potentially inconsistent would cast a pall over the past forty years of intellectual history, since the issue is precisely the one debated in the early years of the Keynesian Revolution under the general label of Keynes vs. The Classics. Writing doctrinal history with an eye to progress and synthesis becomes difficult if progress was absent and synthesis is logically impossible.

For the three groups then, microeconomists, macroeconomists, and historians of economics, there are somewhat different points of entry into the microfoundations of macroeconomics literature, and somewhat different concerns will shape their questions and guide their intuition. Further, they each bring different preconceptions to the analysis and they are likely to construe similar arguments differently. When we understand these viewpoints, it will be an easier task to see the intellectual antecedents of current microfoundations work. It will thus be easier to assay the potential fertility of certain lines of argument, for the manner in which an economist approaches a particular problem will frequently determine the answers that emerge.

A microeconomic perspective

Much of the microfoundations literature rests on the shared perspective of microeconomists that economics is a study of constrained choice in a variety of circumstances. Leaving for the next chapter the historical development of these concerns, it will suffice here to indicate how this viewpoint has shaped the literature.

The world of the microeconomist is peopled with disaggregated individual units (households and firms) and guided by the specification of their decision calculus and resulting interactions. All economic activity leads to the ultimate satisfaction of the households' wants. Each household is a receiver of consumer goods and a provider of labor and capital services for which it is paid an income which constrains its ability to achieve specific levels of satisfaction. The theory of consumer behavior itself is a well-detailed and robust set of assumptions, propositions, and inferences which have led over time to various insights about both traditional market phenomena and observable behaviors not always studied in economic terms (e.g., fertility, education, etc.).

As a consequence of this ability to predict novel facts and relate them to an established disciplinary corpus, the theory of consumer behavior, at the microeconomic level, provides a ready source of modelling techniques potentially applicable to topics of a more highly aggregative nature. When these structures are linked to theories of the firm which elucidate the firm's decision calculus as it acts simultaneously in the supply side of the goods market and the demand side of the factor services market, it is clear that the concatenation of households and firms is a first approximation to the kind of economy that macroeconomics studies.

This circular flow analogy is indeed familiar to all macroeconomics students although it developed from the work of general equilibrium theorists. What is worth noting, however, is that while macroeconomics self-consciously attempts analysis of the economy as a whole, the general equilibrium approach to economic analysis, which studies the interdependent choice problem for various types of economic agents, shares a like concern for holistic reasoning. In particular, the microeconomic general equilibrium view would implicitly deny that aggregative *theorizing* could provide any significant insight that was *logically* unattainable from a more rigorous disaggregative approach.

To be sure, for empirical work one needs to aggregate at least to individual markets and probably beyond (for example, *the* labor market), but in principle no interconnection should appear in a macromodel which is not already present in the underlying general equilibrium structure. For the microeconomists, macroeconomic analysis is at best a useful method for studying directly the problem of immediate concern. It is, under this interpretation however, merely a first step towards a more sophisticated and rigorous modelling procedure which would embed that problem in the disaggregated structure of the basic interrelated units.

For example, macro reasoning which attempts to establish the existence or non-existence of a "liquidity trap" would be useful in two ways: first, empirical studies would help determine whether the phenomenon is "observable" and thus worth explaining and second, aggregative reasoning could suggest the sectoral linkages that would probably be involved in any explanation. The theorist would not consider the phenomenon to have been explained until there existed reasonable and coherent assumptions about the behavior of, and interrelationships among, the atomistic agents which would generate the potentially observable behaviors. For the "liquidity trap," he would add money and bonds and future decision periods. The proposition to be established would be something like "what characteristics of this complicated world entail insensitivity of the demand for money to changes in the interest rate?"

One should not infer arrogance among general equilibrium theorists: their understanding of money, bonds, and intertemporal choice in a monetary economy will be shaped almost totally by the more sophisticated, although more aggregated understandings of macro-monetary theorists. No general equilibrium modelling directed to "liquidity trap" problems would gain assent if, for example, it were assumed that bonds could trade against goods in each period, or that money did not mediate in exchange.

What is being suggested is that for economists whose perspective is microeconomic, scepticism about macroeconomic analysis can only be removed by the process of embedding macroeconomic concerns in a reasonably complete and rigorous general equilibrium system in which the behaviors can be clearly identified and the linkages clearly understood. Explanations of money wage changes in macroeconomic models which are based entirely on labor market excess demands, for instance, will be totally unsatisfactory, mere hand-waving, to the extent that households and firms are not involved and interrelated in the wage determination process.

In this fashion it may be imagined that both "pure" (theoretical) and "applied" (econometric) macroeconomists are scouts for the headquarters of general equilibrium theory; they bring back information about the outline and details of new terrain. Their reports are preliminary only and are not judged to be accurate until the maps are drawn to consistent scale and the headquarters staff can send a second scout party to a precise spot for a definite purpose.

But how do the macro predictions get generated from a general equilibrium structure? What is the internal logic of the approach? Full and detailed answers will have to be postponed for several chapters, but some of the ideas may be sketched. An economy is described by specifying the agents and their behavioral characteristics (preferences), and a state of the economy is characterized by the data, usually some set of prices and quantities, which generate agent behavior. If some state of the economy induces the agents to behave in a coherent manner, that state is said to be an equilibrium. That is, an equilibrium may be (for some models) some set of prices which will, were all agents to act taking those prices as given, generate market outcomes (agent interactions) that produce those same prices.

In this sense the existence of an equilibrium is equivalent to the possibility of pre-reconciled choice. Equilibrium is a set of plans such that (1) for each agent, its plan seems best to it, (2) all plans are consistent among agents, and (3) actions based on those plans induce a well-defined outcome.

If an equilibrium exists, it may be possible to describe its properties using model-extrinsic categories: it may be "efficient," it may involve a particular relationship between the price of bonds and the expectations which link the periods, etc. If the equilibrium is, in addition, robust in the sense that departures from equilibrium set up forces to restore that equilibrium, then comparative static analysis can be applied. Thus it can be learned how, for example, the price of bonds, or the amount of money agents will wish to carry from period to period, will vary if the initial stock of money, or the initial structure of expectations, is changed.

These exercises are precisely the content of the standard macro-economics which would work at a much more aggregative level to examine how an increase in the money supply, *ceteris paribus*, changes the level of real output in an economy. The specification of this exercise in general equilibrium language lays bare the implicit assumptions of the macroeconomic analysis and reveals the complex interactive structure that underlies the "causal" reasoning.

To a microeconomic theorist, then, a study of the microfoundations of macroeconomics is coextensive with general equilibrium analysis. Richer and more detailed specifications of the disaggregated inter-agent framework lead naturally to macroeconomic propositions. To the extent that those theorems replicate the structure revealed in a more aggregated, less "rigorous" macro-analysis, that macroeconomic proposition can be said to have been provided with a logical foundation.

The research program implicit here will be one of extension of some basic general equilibrium structures. Problems within this program involve the suitability of a particular disaggregated structure, the logical coherence of the various component pieces, and the interaction between the modes of reasonable new modelling and the internal logic of the existing models. The "microfoundations of macroeconomics" from this perspective are well-established and reasonably well-understood. Much of the work to be surveyed later is in this tradition, and it will be necessary later to examine it quite critically, for if there are logical defects in this research program, much past and current work has to be abandoned.

Perspective from macroeconomics

A macroeconomic theorist might perceive the microfoundations issue differently. Although it would be granted that a general equilibrium perspective is necessary for an integrated view of economic processes, the market interrelationship would occur at a highly aggregated level, as in the familiar Hicks–Hansen four quadrant (market) analysis.

The primary set of concerns involves explanations of levels and changes in aggregate measures of economic activity: unemployment, inflation, growth, capacity, trade balances, consumption, debt and the like. Theories are articulated at the aggregate level and are tested by aggregate data. It is recognized, of course, that there are dangers in treating sectors (capital goods industries) as though they were monolithic entities but it is usually argued (or assumed) that sectoral behaviors are no more or less complicated than those of the component firms.

In this sense macroeconomic analysis is rather Marshallian with representative firms or households assumed to be aggregates of the atomistic structure which supports the conception. There is an implicit denial that a disaggregated model can support predictions of macro-behavior. Macroeconomists would be uneasy arguing that investment sector behavior is the *net* result of firm A acting to increase investment as the interest rate increases while firm B reduces investment demand by a greater amount than A increased demand.

One result of this shared vision among macroeconomic theorists is that various controversies are adjudicated on fairly limited criteria. The demand for money literature, for example, used various macroeconomic arguments to construct alternative theories which were to explain the determinants of the demand for real money balances. Inventory theoretic reasoning and traditional consumer behavior supported the use of real income as an explanatory variable, portfolio choice supported the real rate of interest, etc. Monetarist and fiscalist positions then got curiously joined to beliefs about the interest elasticity of the money demand and, since perfect inelasticity was never to be found, arguments degenerated into "how inelastic did demand have to be to support a monetarist position?"

For other macroeconomists, there is a philosophic bias against the use of individualistic general equilibrium models to support aggregative theorizing. In particular, those economists who consider themselves followers of Keynes, not his popularizers, i.e., those whom Kregel calls Post-Keynesians, have continued to argue that there are logical incompatibilities between standard general equilibrium theory and the economics of Keynes. If this is granted, then it follows that microfoundations issues take on an entirely new meaning.

As an example of this, consider the role that expectations play in both Keynes' work and general equilibrium analysis. For Keynes, the state of long-term expectations was the major factor determining the marginal efficiency of capital, since a capital good would, by reason of its durability, yield services far into the future. Consequently the demand price of a piece of new capital equipment depends on the pattern of expectations of future yields, or net returns, discounted by an index of a "safe" rate of return on bonds.

One problem, for Keynes, was that there could be no consistent set of expectations of those future yields, since consistency requires that each prospective yield be weighted by the expectation of that yield: producers would, by standard logic, be forced to give point probability estimates of the likelihood of earthquakes twenty years in the future. One must recognize that probability theory models repeated trial situations, and logical difficulties exist if one uses the language of the casino as a guide to action. As a consequence the demand price of capital goods is a convention subject to the psychology of mood and mass behavior and thus is an unstable, or highly volatile, function of its other arguments like the interest rate on bonds.

For most general equilibrium models, however, individuals are supposed to be able to hold expectations of at least the next period's price structure, and those expectations are consistent with the mathematics of probability theory. In models of the capital goods markets we find that all goods are usually lumped together; assets consist usually of money and bonds, and sometimes "ownership shares" of existing plant and equipment which can be traded in dated markets. The expectations are at best those which Keynes called short-term: current producer and consumer expectations of the price at which finished goods can be sold. Keynes was sufficiently unimpressed with the difference *these* expectations made to his overall conception that he assumed that current prices could act as a proxy for these expected prices with no great analytic harm.

The difficulty is clear. The sort of expectations that Keynes felt were important have not been, and some would argue cannot be, modelled in a disaggregated general equilibrium system. Consequently, that system necessarily assumes we have a knowledge of the future quite different from that which we ordinarily possess, and it cannot be "aggregated up" to Keynes' system.

For Post-Keynesian macrotheorists the microfoundations problem is a problem of microeconomics. Its language, conceptual categories, and intellectual underpinnings are too limited to support sophisticated macroeconomic reasoning. Some Post-Keynesians believe that it has been a lack of attention to such matters by general equilibrium theorists that has induced the micro–macro split, while others argue that the split is a *logical* problem, incapable of resolution without abandoning either general equilibrium theory or Post-Keynesian economics.

On either view, they consider macroeconomics to have been cut free, by Keynes, from standard microeconomic analysis and consequently the way is open to them to reconstitute microtheory to support explicit Post-Keynesian analysis. From such a perspective the problem of "what microfoundations for macroeconomics?" becomes an extrapolation of macroeconomic reasoning back to the behavior of individual units.

For example, it is well-known that aggregate data support the observation that the price level tends to move with unit labor costs or, more precisely, the rate of price inflation is directly proportional to the difference between the rate of wage inflation and the rate of change of average labor productivity. For Post-Keynesian macroeconomics, an agenda item for research is thus to provide a microeconomic explanation of this "aggregate mark-up" relationship, to explain why it should hold at an aggregated level.

If one grants that the relationship is not accidental, and one supposes that the searchers are not being misled by *post hoc, ergo propter hoc* reasoning, there are many preliminary microeconomic hypotheses to be explored. The explanation which seems to have commanded widest assent here appears to involve the relative importance of large industrial firms, and unions, in modern capitalistic economies. Such firms, it is argued, are demand-generating rather than demand-constrained and they have considerable monopoly power. Large unions, in bargaining over wages with these firms, generate changes in money wages in amount best explained by habit, relative power, and other socio-economic factors. The firms, observing the level of average labor productivity, then adjust their prices upward to preserve the mark-ups which generate enough corporate profits to (*a*) keep shareholders from complaining and (*b*) provide sufficient internal finance to expand plant and equipment. Smaller firms then raise prices too since their costs are now higher and their perceived demand is greater (since workers in the large firms have increased money incomes to spend).

This reasoning is crude by the standards of rigor found in general equilibrium theory, but it does "support" the macroeconomic reasoning. Further, it cannot be evaluated from the traditional microeconomic perspective since many of the questions it raises appear to be ideological. In any event, assumptions about the behavior of large firms are irrelevant to a discrimination between the theories. The test is their predictive power and consistency with other established theoretical linkages. This criterion, though, is moot since Post-Keynesian microtheory is, by its own supporters, supposed to be considered apart from the "neoclassical" categories.

It ought to be apparent that for at least some macroeconomists the microfoundations literature must be different from general equilibrium theory. What appears to be an agenda item for one group will appear to be irrelevant to the other's concerns. It is this tension which gives importance to the topic, for as long as there continues to be fundamental disagreement about the basic structure of economic theory, there will be continued disagreement about many matters of practical economic importance.

The doctrine-historical perspective

Recent years bear witness to a new concern with the internal logic of economic discovery. Rational reconstruction of developments within the discipline has led a number of economists to Imre Lakatos' view that scientific progress can be fruitfully analyzed using the methodology of scientific research programs (MSRP) [Lakatos, 1970].

Without here attempting a full survey of these ideas, in essence the MSRP approach suggests that at the heart of a discipline there exists a *hard core* of propositions, assumptions, and beliefs that are taken as irrefutable by all members of the scientific community in question. Linked to this hard core is the *protective belt* of the standard corpus of scientific analysis, in which particular theories and models of the discipline reside. Since associated with the hard core is a *positive heuristic* which directs scientific investigators towards certain questions, and a *negative heuristic* which rules out certain investigations as nonscientific, scientific progress occurs in the protective belt of a research program.

The reader will not be misled by the use of Lakatos' terminology in this study if the fundamental idea is granted, namely that progress in a discipline is better described by a sequence of theories, or models, not by a study of individual theories. A "research program" is the organizing conception; to describe it is to characterize the various sequences of models that have a family resemblance. The MSRP approach thus investigates both what is common to elements of the sequence and what makes one theory in the sequence change into another.

The liberties taken here with Lakatos' terminology are dangerous to his conception; economists have by now reduced Kuhn's "paradigm" to the status of a "buzz-word." Our use of some language from the philosophy of science can be recognized in

Leijonhufvud's remark that the effort "is obviously philosophically amateurish. It cannot be overlooked, but I trust it will be forgiven. It is, in any case, the price philosophers will have to pay for cooperation of economists" [Leijonhufvud, 1976, p. 65].

A *progressive* research program is thus best thought of as hard core and a succession of theories which, when generated by that hard core, have the power to predict novel facts, explain anomalies, and provide an appropriate amount of excess content to structure new investigations. In contradistinction a *degenerative* research program is one in which novel facts and anomalies are explained at the cost of ever-decreasing analytic content and continual *ad hoc* hedging of theories. One can never on this approach falsify a theory, but rather one can evaluate the internal scientific response to anomaly and ask whether it has been characterized by a problem shift that is progressive or degenerative.

Notice that the emergence of a new research program corresponds loosely to the older Kuhnian view of a paradigm-shift, or a revolution.

From this perspective it can be suggested that the decade of the 1930s saw the degenerative Marshallian program replaced with two competing programs, the macroeconomic and microeconomic, or the Keynesian and Hicksian, or as we have already termed them, the Keynesian program and the neo-Walrasian program. Consequently the "microfoundations of macroeconomics" has, as its domain of discourse, the delineation of each program and the interconnections between them. For instance, identification of the respective hard cores would itself lead to an improved understanding of their potential linkages.

The presumption here is that economists should *not* think in terms of simple reductionism of macro to micro, or micro to macro. The logic of competing scientific research programs suggests that, although they each attempt to explain *some* of the same phenomena (i.e., their protective belts overlap to some degree) their incompatible hard cores make unification of their research agendas impossible. Reduction of one to the other would make sense only if one program was degenerating with respect to the other so that the progressive program could generate the empirical content of both and still allow predictions of novel facts.

For a methodologist, then, the microfoundations literature provides case study material, for this century, of changes in economic theory. The emergence of not one but two competing research programs from the wreck of Marshallian analysis is a story which can be used either as a moral cautionary tale or for the sheer drama of the plot itself. In either case, its power on the collective imagination of the economics profession has led to its telling and re-telling; we are still under the spell of those "years of high theory" when giants walked the earth.

That which is to follow

An interest in issues related to the microfoundations of macroeconomics can thus be justified from a variety of perspectives. To follow the emerging literature of the subject, and to document its twists, turns, false starts, and successes, it is necessary to spend some time understanding the antecedents of current work. Consequently, the next chapter will explore the development of neo-Walrasian general equilibrium theory from the 1930s to about 1960. Our interest will be in the progressive nature of the neo-Walrasian research program and the range of its explanatory power.

In Chapter 3 we shall examine the competing program of macroeconomics as it was presented by Keynes in the *General Theory of Employment, Interest, and Money*. Our purpose is only incidentally exegetical. More fundamantally we must ask how it was possible for Keynes' analysis to be so differently reconstituted by neo-Walrasians, Keynesians, and Post-Keynesians. We shall see that Keynes himself laid the groundwork for these varied interpretations of his immense contribution.

In Chapter 4 we shall examine the macroeconomic theory that is entailed by the general equilibrium theory of Chapter 2. Again, the presentation is historical, from 1939 to 1960, as the theory was elaborated by Hicks, Lange, Klein, and Patinkin. Our concern will be to document the macroeconomic lessons that could be drawn from the neo-Walrasian structure, and to circumscribe those purely macroeconomic insights that could not be so "captured." In particular, we shall study some innovations from Keynes' work that were logically incompatible with the general equilibrium analysis of the period, and we shall see how these contributions were treated in the standard literature.

Part I concludes with Chapter 5 in which an alternative view of the microfoundations of macroeconomics, based on the work of Clower and Leijonhufvud, is presented and criticized. The difficulties that earlier works had in articulating the micro–macro relationship will be seen to have developed from a logically flawed view of the foundations issues. A program for putting matters right will be seen to entail significant emendations in neo-Walrasian analysis. Part II will describe various current approaches to such a reformulation, and Part III will offer a brief conclusion.

2

Development of the neo-Walrasian program: 1930-60

"in reality the economic system is a whole of which all the parts are connected and react on each other . . . It seems, therefore, as if, for a complete and rigorous solution of the problems relative to some parts of the economic system, it were indispensable to take the entire system into consideration. But this would surpass the powers of mathematical analysis and of our practical methods of calculation" [Cournot, 1838, p. 198].

The precursors: equilibrium

Although Cournot's insight remained largely unexplored until Walras, the modern developments of the theory probably proceed from Gustav Cassel. In his *Theory of the Social Economy* he set out in a tractable form a simplified Walrasian system and noted that "the pricing problem is essentially a single problem extending over the whole of the exchange economy and [this fact] gives the pricing prices process an intrinsic consistency which can only be expressed by a system of simultaneous equations" [Cassell, 1932, p. 148].

The analysis was straightforward even by modern standards although the mathematics was used more to achieve expositional clarity than to uncover new features of the system. It was as if economists had to agree on the modelling procedures, the structure of the problem, before mathematical analysis could be utilized.

Current understanding takes the general equilibrium problem as: (*a*) to provide models of private ownership economic systems in which the interdependence of producing and consuming economic agents is identified; (*b*) to explicate those choices which the agents make independently; (*c*) to identify the role of the price system in mediating the potentially conflicting choices made by the agents; and (*d*) to assess the robustness of constructions which "solve" problems (*a*)–(*c*).

If this is granted, Cassel certainly tackled (*a*), partially analyzed (*b*), and discussed in a non-rigorous fashion (*c*) and, to a lesser degree, (*d*).

The Walras–Cassel system was thus "ripe" for solution, and most of the modern analysis was initiated in a series of papers generated by discussions in the early 1930s in Menger's seminar in Vienna.[1] More precisely, Wald's [1936] paper reported the first true solution of the general equilibrium problem in the sense of (*a*)–(*d*) above.

Wald's exchange economy was described by n individuals, m commodities, and initial stocks a_{ij} = amount of good j initially held by individual i. Preferences were "given" by well-behaved indifference surfaces and the equation system was a set of equilibrium conditions involving price: marginal utility ratios for all goods for all individuals, and individual budget constraints.

If $x_1, \ldots, x_m$ are amounts of the various commodities, and U_i is utility for individual i, it is possible to define

$$f_{ij}(x_1, \ldots, x_m) \equiv \lambda_i(x_1, \ldots, x_m) \frac{\partial U_i(x_1, \ldots, x_m)}{\partial x_j} \quad (j = 1, 2, \ldots, m)$$

so that f_{ij} is (up to proportionality $= \lambda$) simply a marginal utility function.[2]

---

[1] For some source material on Karl Menger (mathematician son of the 19th century economist) and this famous seminar, see Baumol and Goldfeld (1968), especially pp. 267–71.

[2] The constant λ results from the fact the indifference curves are assumed given. Integrating back to get utilities introduces integration constants.

Wald's theorem then stated that the exchange equations had at least one solution for the relative prices $p_2, p_3, \ldots, p_m$ ($p_1 = 1$, as numeraire) and Δa_{ij} for all i and j, and $p_j > 0$ with $a_{ij} + \Delta a_{ij} \geq 0$ provided:

(1) $a_{ij} \geq 0$ for all i,j (so that no person holds negative stocks)

(2) $\sum_i a_{ij} > 0$ for all j (there are positive stocks of each good)

(3) $\sum_j a_{ij} > 0$ for all i (each individual has a positive endowment) and

(4) $f_{ij}(x_1, \ldots, x_m)$ is of the form $f_i(x_1, \ldots, x_m)\, \varphi_{ij}(x_j)$ for all i, j where f_i is any non-zero function and φ_{ij} is continuous monotone decreasing. (Essentially, this says that diminishing marginal utility prevails.)

> Conditions 1 to 4, which prove the solubility of the equations of exchange, agree substantially with the Walrasian assumptions. Thus Walras is correct in asserting the solubility of his equations of exchange. However, this can only be proven with the aid of recondite methods of modern mathematics, and the method Walras uses to attempt to prove the existence of equilibrium prices is completely inadequate [Wald, 1951, p. 384].

The first modern existence proof had little effect on English speaking economists. The proofs themselves have only recently been translated from the original German [Baumol and Goldfeld, 1968]. The survey article in which the results were simply reported was not translated into English until Wald's death in 1951. The reasons for the neglect are not hard to understand. The year 1936 was not one in which the best professional economists were intellectually restless and looking for recondite problems to study: the *General Theory* took care of that. Further, even if the German language had been accessible, the mathematics was forbidding and the Vienna group itself was breaking up under the Hitler madness.

But if it had been recognized at the time that Wald had solved the general equilibrium problem that Walras and Cassel had structured, it was not perceived that such systems had any real macroeconomic content. Indeed, Keynes was suggesting that aggregate supply and demand analysis had few roots in the traditional theory of value once the economy was to exist in historical time. The formal apparatus of general equilibrium theory worked at best with a constant-coefficient technology and numeraire money. Keynes' monetary theory of production was hardly reconcilable with this conception, and few economists thought such a reconciliation could be interesting.

The only other rigorous treatment of existence of solutions of general equilibrium models was John von Neumann's "A Model of General Economic Equilibrium." This paper too came out of Menger's seminar and appeared in German in 1937 although it was "read for the first time in the winter of 1932 at the mathematical seminar of Princeton University" [Von Neumann, 1945, p. 1].

Von Neumann considered an economy with growing factors of production and a fixed constant-returns technology which produced n goods by means of m processes. The problem was to determine the m process intensities, the growth rate, the n prices of goods, and the interest rate. A number of economic assumptions (subsistence wages, possibility of free goods, indecomposability etc.) were imposed to ensure existence of a balanced growth path or equilibrium. The proof technique used both mini–max arguments and the Brouwer fixed-point theorem.

This short paper was a remarkable tour de force and started developments in three distinct theoretical areas: (1) activity analysis models of production; (2) non-aggregative capital theory; and (3) existence of competitive equilibria.

It is (3) which is of concern here. The paper set out in sensible form the major issues of general equilibrium theory in a way which sacrificed no rigor to intuition. The inequality constraints forced awareness of the "free goods" problem and the role of scarcity in a modern manner. The use of fixed-point arguments presaged a literature twenty years unborn; the understanding of the interplay between tools and reasoning set a tone for subsequent analyses.

By the end of the 1930s, then, there did exist rigorous and detailed equilibrium models of the Walrasian system. These models were not generally accessible to most economists though they could hardly have been called "lost gems." The problems they investigated were not yet connected to the growing literature on macroeconomics and monetary theory. A revolution (à la Keynes) was at hand and Cambridge and London were under siege. English speaking economists may be forgiven for slighting the unheralded revolution in Vienna.

Dynamic processes: early work[3]

Although there were economists, in the 1930s and before, who took a great deal of care to distinguish between "equilibria" and "stability," it was Samuelson who actually provided economists with both the taxonomy and analysis of these terms for the first time. His *Foundations of Economic Analysis* [1947] was based on several earlier papers which defined an equilibrium state as a state such that certain conditions, called "equilibrium conditions," were satisfied. Since economists were also concerned with comparative statics (how parameter changes affected equilibrium outcomes), a dynamic theory of change was related to any comparative static exercise. Samuelson pointed out that economists had never really taken care to formulate explicit dynamic theories, even though such theories were necessary for comparative static analysis. Without a dynamic adjustment mechanism in the form of a law of motion for the system being considered, no comparative static argument could be valid. An unstable system which was subject to a parameter change would not necessarily arrive at that "new" equilibrium which was to have been compared with the old; stability analysis logically preceded comparative statics.

The implications for Walrasian general equilibrium were apparent. The Walrasian system at that time was actually a specification of a large number of equilibrium conditions in the form of statements that supply must be equal to demand in every market. These conditions came from (1) utility maximization by consumers

---

[3] Some material in this section is based on Weintraub, E. R., "General Equilibrium Theory," Chapter 6 in S. Weintraub [ed] *Modern Economic Thought* (Philadelphia; University of Pennsylvania Press, 1976).

and (2) profit maximization by competitive firms. The Wald analysis entailed, with common sense restrictions on the form of the functions, that an equilibrium set of market-clearing prices "existed." What, however, was the mechanism by which prices changed? The absence of such an adjustment process precluded any discussion of stability and thus of comparative statics.

Earlier authors, like Hicks, had defined stability and instability and thereafter used these definitions to classify equilibria. The Walrasian equilibrium conditions could be written as

$$D_i(p_1, \ldots, p_n) - S_i(p_1, \ldots, p_n) = 0, \qquad i = 1, 2, \ldots, n \qquad (1)$$

or

$$E_i(p_1, \ldots, p_n) = 0, \qquad i = 1, 2, \ldots, n \qquad (2)$$

where $p_i = i$th price and D_i, S_i, and E_i are demand for, supply of, and excess demand for the ith commodity respectively.

Hicks considered the Jacobian matrix[4]

$$\left(\frac{dE_i}{dp_j} \right) \quad i, j = 1, 2, \ldots, n \qquad (3)$$

of system (2), and defined perfect stability to mean that the principal minors (of the determinant) of matrix (3) alternated in sign,
i.e.

$$\det \left(\frac{dE_1}{dp_1} \right) < 0, \quad \det \begin{pmatrix} \dfrac{dE_1}{dp_1} & \dfrac{dE_1}{dp_2} \\ \dfrac{dE_2}{dp_1} & \dfrac{dE_2}{dp_2} \end{pmatrix} > 0, \text{ etc.} \qquad (4)$$

Such a definition depended *only* on system (2) and did not utilize any dynamic adjustment process. For a single market, with linear demand and supply schedules, it simply reduced to the elementary statement that

$$\text{slope of demand curve} < \text{slope of supply curve}, \qquad (5)$$

---

[4] Thus dE_i/dp_j, if positive, expresses gross substitutability between goods i and j, since it states that excess demand for i increases if j's price increases.

or that the supply curve cut the demand curve from below.

Samuelson followed a well-established literature in mathematics when he formulated the definition of stability with reference to a given dynamic system. An equilibrium was stable if it was "attracting"; that is, deviations from the equilibrium were eliminated by the dynamic laws of motion. To equilibrium conditions like (2), one must append a dynamic model like the tatonnement:

$$\frac{\mathrm{d}p_i}{\mathrm{d}t} = k_i \, \mathrm{E}_i(p_1, \ldots, p_n), \qquad i = 1, 2, \ldots, n \tag{6}$$

which states that the rate of change of the ith price is proportionate to excess demand in the ith market. In the case of linear systems (linear excess demand functions) Samuelson was able, by a straightforward application of some other mathematical theorems, to provide necessary and sufficient conditions for stability of equilibrium. To see this, linearize (6) to give

$$\frac{\mathrm{d}p_i}{\mathrm{d}t} = k_i \, (a_i + b_{ij} \, p_j) \qquad i = 1, 2, \ldots, n \tag{7}$$

which can be written compactly in vector–matrix form as

$$\frac{\mathrm{d}p}{\mathrm{d}t} = Ka + KBp \tag{8}$$

Where $p = (p_1, \ldots, p_n)^T$, $K = \mathrm{diag}(k_1, k_2, \ldots, k_n)$, $a = (a_1, \ldots, a_n)^T$, $B = (b_{ij})$. ("T" denotes the transpose operator.)

Samuelson took $K = \mathrm{diag} \, (1, 1, \ldots, 1)$ and found that the Walrasian equilibrium (solution of (2)) was stable *if and only if* the eigenvalues of the matrix B had negative real parts. This too entailed that stability in a single market (for $B = (b)$) depended on a negative slope of the excess demand function, or (5), the Hicks result. In brief, Samuelson's definition of dynamic stability yielded, for linear systems, necessary and sufficient conditions for stability based on a *mathematical* property of the Jacobian of the excess demand function. In general, this property had no economic interpretation, while Hicks' definition yielded a characterization of stability that seemed to have economic content, since the Jacobian's having alternating minors was a sufficient condition for solution of a class of optimization problems.

The next problem was to characterize conditions, preferably with essential economic content, under which the "true" Samuelson definition was equivalent to the "intuitively sensible" Hicks criterion.

Answers were provided by Smithies [1942] and Metzler [1945]. Smithies was first able to show that in some cases economic meaning could be given to the eigenvalue type of stability condition. Metzler's paper settled the matter in a most elegant fashion when he demonstrated the equivalence of the Samuelson and Hicks formulations under various alternative conditions. For example,

(*a*) If, in (8), $k = \text{diag}(1,1, \ldots, 1)$, then Hicks' definition is entailed by Samuelson's, or

(*b*) If all goods are strong gross substitutes (i.e., $\mathrm{d}E_i/\mathrm{d}p_j > 0$; $i \neq j$) then Hicks' and Samuelson's definitions are equivalent.

It is important to recognize just how limited a set of propositions these were. They dealt with "given excess demand functions," as in (6). They did not use any economic hypothesis to cut down the number of possible functions E_i which appeared; consequently there was not much in the *economics* of the problem, except strong gross substitutability, which was a recognizable stabilizer. The assumption that excess demand functions were linear was crucial to the "true" dynamic stability characterization. Even though stability was *defined* for arbitrary processes like (6), results could only be obtained for linear systems like (8). This was useful since *instability* for (8) entailed *instability* for (6), but the important problem was to present *economic* assumptions which entailed stability of (6). Such theorems were not easy: it would be almost fifteen years before economists could solve the problem.

By the late 1940s, then, the original Walras–Cassel system had been articulated with reasonable care. Although Wald had presented a proof of existence of equilibrium, his assumptions were designed to ensure mathematical tractability. Stability or robustness arguments based on the economic properties of the system were non-existent although several preliminary steps had been taken. The stage was set for the rapid and imaginative developments of the 1950s.

The Arrow–Debreu–McKenzie Model

The modern era in general equilibrium theory began in 1954, for in that year Arrow and Debreu remodelled the Wald system by introducing production sets and preference structures to replace "fixed-coefficient" technologies and marginal utility functions. Other papers by McKenzie [1959], Gale [1955], et al., provided a rigorous treatment of a disaggregated private ownership economy.

This model (which we shall abbreviate as the ADM model)[5] is the foundation for much current work; modifications, extensions, and criticisms of the ADM model are the basis of what we have termed the neo-Walrasian research program. It is thus necessary to linger a bit over the details of this structure, for our understanding of much current work will depend on familiarity with the component parts and internal logic of the ADM conception.

If any single work in this area can be considered canonical, it is Debreu's *Theory of Value* [1959]. We adopt (for the time being) Debreu's notation and suppose that m = number of consumers, n = number of producers, and l = number of commodities, all finite, We define $X_i \subset R^l$ to be the ith consumer's consumption set, with typical element x_i (an l-vector) and $Y_i \subset R^l$ to be the jth producer's production set with typical element y_j (an l-vector). $w \in R^l$ is a point (l-vector) describing the economy's total (given) resources. Each vector of l components thus represents a "basket" or "bundle" of goods. Representing goods bundles as points in Euclidean l-space implies that, for instance, commodities can be as divisible, and homogeneous, as space itself.

An *economy*, E, is given by:

(1) a non-empty set $X_i \subset R^l$ where a relation $\succsim_i$ for $i = 1,2,\ldots,n$

---

[5] Many authors use the term Arrow–Debreu model. Since, however, the *proof* of existence on which current work is based came out of McKenzie [1959], it seems appropriate to give McKenzie equal billing.

is given on X_i. $\succsim_i$ is a complete quasi-order. This relation, which is a primitive for each individual, is read "at least as desirable as" so that $x \succsim_i y$ reads "for individual i, bundle x is at least as desirable as bundle y." Completeness means that *any* pair of bundles x and y can be compared by any individual. A quasi-ordering also requires (1) that if x is at least as desirable as y, and y is at least as desirable as z, then x is at least as desirable as z (transitivity); (2) x is at least as desirable as x (reflexivity); and (3) if x is at least as desirable as y, and z is a bundle "almost" identical to x, then z is at least as desirable as y (continuity).

(2) a non-empty set $Y_j \subset R^l$

(3) a point $w \in R^l$.

A *state* of an economy E is an $(m + n)$-tuple (i.e., a vector of consumption vectors and production vectors, one for each consumer and producer) $(x_1, \ldots, x_m, y_1, \ldots, y_n)$ where each x_i and y_j are l-vectors. Aggregating consumptions and productions so that $y = \sum\limits_{j=1}^{n} y_j$ and $x = \sum\limits_{j=1}^{m} x_j$ we have $z = x - y - w \equiv$ excess demand.

A market *equilibrium* for E is a state of E (i.e., a combination of an x, a y, and a w) such that $z = 0$.

Taken together the assumptions suggest that goods are finite in number and completely divisible. Consumers have sensible preference structures, and resources are given to the economy. An equilibrium state for the economy is one such that the net demands exhaust the available resources.

For a private ownership economy ε, there is the additional complication that consumers own the resources and receive the production profits. Thus let $w_i =$ resources owned by consumer i (so that $w = \sum\limits_{i=1}^{m} w_i$) for $w_i \in R^l$, and $\theta_{ij} =$ share of profit of firm j owned by consumer i (with $\theta_{ij} \geqslant 0$ and $\sum\limits_{i=1}^{m} \theta_{ij} = 1$).

The basic ADM model is that of a *private ownership economy ε* which is given by:

(1′) an economy $((X_i, \succsim_i), Y_j, w)$ (i.e., a consumption set and a preference relation for each consumer, a production set for each producer, and a bundle of resource endowments)

(2′) for each i, a point $w_i \in R^l$ such that $\sum\limits_{i=1}^{m} w_i = w$ (so that consumers "own" the resources)

(3′) for each pair (i,j) a non-negative real number θ_{ij} such that for each j, $\sum\limits_{i=1}^{m} \theta_{ij} = 1$ (so that firms are "owned" by consumers)

An equilibrium of ε is an $(m + n + 1)$-tuple $((x_i^*), (y_j^*), p^*)$ of points in R^l (so that each *point* is a vector) such that

(a) x_i^* is maximal in $\{x_i \in X_i : p^* x_i \leqslant p^* w + \sum\limits_{j=1}^{n} \theta_{ij} p^* y_j^*\}$

with respect to $\succsim_i$ for every i,j; that is, for each individual i, x_i^* is that bundle, among all consumption bundles which are affordable (expenditures on them do not exceed income), which is most desirable.

(β) y_j^* maximizes profit relative to p^* on Y_j, for every j

(γ) $x^* - y^* = w^*$.

An equilibrium can be thought of as a set of non-negative prices, one for each of the l goods, such that if consumers and producers were each individually to optimize taking those prices as given, the resulting market demand and supply quantities would just balance and would yield market prices identical to those taken as "given." *Existence of equilibrium is thus equivalent to the logical possibility of pre-reconcilable choices.*

Phrased in this manner, there is a straightforward heuristic for a proof. Consider a non-negative price vector p. For these prices, let each consumer and producer optimize. Now the market quantities which result generate an excess demand or supply in each of the l markets. If there is an excess demand in market i, increase the ith component of p, if excess supply obtains, reduce that price. We thus obtain a new price vector, p'. With the resulting p', repeat the previous experiment to get p''. Under what conditions will this process of "fudging" p terminate? Are there reasonable economic restrictions on consumer and producer behavior that produce a price vector which will clear all markets simultaneously?

Speaking somewhat more precisely, it is clear that we can look at relative prices, or that we can take $p_1 + p_2 + \ldots + p_l = 1$. A price vector thus "lives" in the unit l-simplex (unit "triangle" in l-space). Our heuristic starts with a point in that simplex and generates market excess demands. There is thus a point-to-set mapping, or correspondence, of a price and the associated non-empty set of "excess demands compatible with the selection by every consumer of a consumption optimal for his wealth constraint and by every producer of a production optimal for that price system ... The correspondence ... is called the excess demand correspondence" [Debreu, 1959, p. 80]. Since that excess demand is consistent with a *set* of prices in the simplex, we in fact have a point to set mapping from the set of prices to itself. This idea is a tricky one. Since we have *not* assumed that indifference curves, for example, are strictly convex, it is possible for there to be flat segments on them. If the budget line, or income constraint, is parallel to this flat segment, it is clear that a multiplicity of consumption bundles would be consistent with the given price ratio, because a tangency solution gives, not a point, but a line segment. Since each of these bundles would have been *produced* at a different price ratio, a mapping from prices to consumptions to compatible productions back to prices starts from a price vector (a point) and ends up with a *set* of price vectors. If there was some price which generated excess demands which would produce market outcomes compatible only with that original price, equilibrium is established. Does there exist some price which gets mapped to itself via the correspondence?

The formal problem thus becomes one of establishing a fixed-point for the excess demand correspondence. Existence of fixed points of mappings certainly requires information on the mapping itself, that is, the various sets which play a role in the construction of the correspondence. Thus proofs of existence of equilibrium for private ownership economies will involve various restrictions on consumption sets and production sets.

For Debreu, the problem was reduced to the following *Theorem*: The private ownership economy $\varepsilon = ((X_i, \succsim_i), Y_j, w_i, \theta_{ij})$ has an equilibrium if, for every $i = 1, 2, \ldots, m$

(a) X_i is closed, convex, and has a lower bound for $\leqq$
(b) there is no satiation consumption in X_i
(c) for every x_i' in X_i, the sets $\{x_i \in X_i : x_i \succsim_i x_i'\}$ and $\{x_i \in X_i : x_i \precsim_i x_i'\}$ are closed in X_i
(d) if x_i^1 and x_i^2 are two points in X_i and $t \in (0,1)$ then $x_i^2 \succsim_i x_i^1$ implies $t x_i^2 + (1 - t) x_i^1 \succsim_i x_i^1$
(e) there is an x_i^0 in X_i such that $x_i^0 \ll w_i$ for all i and for every $j = 1, 2, \ldots, n$
(f) $0 \in Y_j$
(g) Y is closed and convex
(h) $Y \cap (-Y) \supset \{0\}$
(i) $Y \supset (-\Omega)$ where $-\Omega$ is the negative orthant.

The importance of this theorem requires that the mathematics not be permitted to obscure the main ideas. Verbally, the assumptions suggest that, given a private ownership economy, with many consumers having reasonable preference orderings, producers having available technologies, and positive stocks of resources, an equilibrium price vector exists provided

(a) The consumption set is "nice." That is, the limit of a sequence of feasible consumption bundles is, itself, a feasible bundle. Convex combinations of feasible bundles are feasible, and there is a "worst" bundle.
(b) For any feasible consumption bundle, there is another such bundle containing more "stuff."
(c) If, for individual i, there is a sequence of feasible bundles, all at least as desirable as bundle x^1, then the limit of that sequence is also a feasible bundle at least as desirable as x^1.
(d) If individual i considers x^2 at least as desirable a bundle as x^1, then any convex combination of x^2 and x^1 must also be considered at least as desirable as x^1.
(e) For every individual i, and every commodity j, there is some

feasible consumption of good j which is less than the endowment of good j by person i.

(f) Any producer, like the jth, always has the opportunity to use no inputs to produce nothing.

(g) The limit of a sequence of feasible productions is also a feasible production; production is not subject to increasing returns.

(h) Production is irreversible.

(i) Free production is impossible (i.e., it requires inputs to produce outputs).

This theorem is the cornerstone of modern general equilibrium theory, and as we shall see later much current work has developed from it. Extension and refinements of the model consider externalities in consumption and production, increasing returns, interdependent choice, stochastic preferences, uncertainty, several distinct time periods, money, transactions structures, information costs, etc.

Stability theory[6]

With the existence problem "settled" by the late 1950s, mathematical theorists reexamined those issues of dynamic adjustment raised by Hicks, Samuelson, Metzler, et al., in the early 1940s. The research involved: (1) taking an Arrow–Debreu representation of the Walrasian system, (2) modelling the tatonnement adjustment process, and (3) finding the *economic* assumptions which would guarantee stability under the tatonnement rules.

As with the existence problem and its solution via fixed-point theorems, stability theory relied on an old mathematical technique which was new to economists, the "second" or "indirect" method of Liapunov [1907].

Consider, for example, the differential equation

$$\dot{x} = f(x), \qquad x(0) = x_0 \tag{9}$$

Here x is a real number, $\dot{x}$ is dx/dt, and f is a very well-behaved (differentiable, say) function. An equilibrium is a function of time

[6] See note 3, p. 23.

(i.e., a state) $x_e(t)$, such that $\dot{x}_e(t) = 0$; alternatively, it is a root or zero of the function $f(x)$. To find out whether a given equilibrium $x_e(t)$ is stable, one needs to examine whether other "nearby" motions of the system "get close" to $x_e(t)$. That is, system (9) says that through every point in the x-plane there is a motion or trajectory or flow determined by (9). Since $x_e(t)$ is a constant motion $(\dot{x}_e(t) = 0)$ we must examine whether motions through points $x(t)$, near $x_e(t)$, themselves become nearly constant.

We are thus led to consider: (*a*) an equilibrium of a system like (9): (*b*) a representation of the *distance* between arbitrary motions of the system and the equilibrium at every instant of time and (*c*) a study of whether, over time, the distance between an arbitrary motion and equilibrium grows smaller; if so, then the system's rules mean that non-equilibrium states approach equilibrium, and thus the equilibrium is stable.

For the tatonnement of equation (8), if p_i is the deviation of the ith price from equilibrium, one gets the system, for $p = (p_1, \ldots, p_n)^T$,

$$\dot{p} = KBp \tag{10}$$

with $p_e = 0$ being the equilibrium. Now certainly $\frac{1}{2} p^T p$ measures half the square of the distance from p to equilibrium, and thus it behaves like distance itself. But

$$\frac{d}{dt} \left(\tfrac{1}{2} p^T p \right) = \tfrac{1}{2}(p^T \dot{p} + \dot{p}^T p)$$

Using $\dot{p}$ from (10) then gives

$$\frac{d}{dt} \left(\tfrac{1}{2} p^T p \right) = \tfrac{1}{2}(p^T KBp + p^T B^T K^T p) = p^T \left(\frac{KB + B^T K^T}{2} \right) p \tag{11}$$

Sufficient conditions for stability are then sufficient conditions that $\frac{d}{dt}$ (distance) < 0, but these are simply conditions that the quadratic form $p^T \dfrac{KB + (KB)^T}{2} p$ be negative definite. Since K represents speeds of adjustment, and B is the Jacobian of the excess demand matrix, whatever conditions on K and B ensure that the quadratic form is negative definite will be *economic* conditions sufficient to guarantee stability of the tatonnement system given by (10).

To get an appreciation of the stability literature, it is useful to see how far this argument can go. If we set $K = \text{diag} (1,1, \ldots, 1)$ so the system of tatonnements is independent of adjustment speeds, stability depends entirely on the Jacobian matrix B of partial derivatives of excess demands with respect to price. For a single market, this matrix is a real number, the slope of the excess demand function, and elementary reasoning shows that the slope must be negative for stability. In an exchange model, with perfectly inelastic supply, this reduces to the statement that the demand curve must slope downward.

If we could imitate this partial result for all markets, we would want all the diagonal elements of B to be negative. Further, it should be the case that the various markets are linked by substitutability relations, since complementarities induce deviation amplifying price swings.

These insights were employed by Arrow and Hurwicz [1958] and McKenzie [1960b] to produce the following

Theorem: For the linear tatonnement system (10), with $K = \text{diag} (1,1, \ldots, 1)$, the equilibrium is asymptotically stable if the excess demand functions are continuously differentiable, are homogeneous of degree zero in prices, satisfy Walras' Law, and exhibit gross substitutability.

Shortly thereafter there appeared a series of papers by Arrow, Block, and Hurwicz [1959], Hahn [1958], Negishi [1958] et al., which removed the restriction of this theorem to linear systems. Thus "nice" excess demand functions from an economist's point of view entailed stability of the tatonnement adjustment process.

These results were soon shown to be about as much as could be hoped for when Scarf [1960] produced a range of interesting classes of "reasonable" economic systems which were *unstable*. These examples "suggest ... [that] instability seems to be a universal phenomenon in competitive economies, rather than an exceptional one, whereas global stability [can be] expected to prevail only in very well-behaved systems," [Nikaido, 1969, p. 337].

The stability problem was thus solved by around 1960 in the sense that there did exist at least one dynamic adjustment mechanism (the tatonnement), and a collection of economic restrictions on systemic behavior, which produced sufficient conditions for stability of equilibrium.

The ADM model was thus "settled" in its articulation and workings although its defects were apparent. In addition to the rigid static structure which was needed to ensure existence of equilibrium, a particularly curious dynamic process was needed to ensure any robustness of that equilibrium. Although the Walrasian "auctioneer" had a long history in such models, he was singularly maladapted to the sort of decentralized decision-making that lay at the center of the static ADM concept. Further, the timeless nature of the process could not be reconciled with those attempts to generalize the ADM model to a multi-period setting. Stability theory was indeed a "collection of sufficient conditions, anecdotes really" [Hahn, 1970] which could potentially distract general equilibrium theorists from more comprehensive investigations.

One way to focus the preceding remarks is through examination of a critique of general equilibrium theory by an "insider" as Janos Kornai describes his considerable credentials as a mathematical economist.

For Kornai, in his book *Anti-Equilibrium*, the primary difficulty of general equilibrium theory is that "The category of phenomena which can be even approximately described by the set of twelve basic assumptions is extremely restricted ... [and the theory] offers little explanation of the real motion of the economy" [p. 30].

The extended critique that Kornai initiates involves examining the ADM model in its 1950s form and finding that (1) its assumptions about optimization behavior are counterfactual, (2) its silence on information flows and control points in a hierarchical economy is misleading, and (3) its lack of institutional detail of how modern economies *actually* allocate goods via non-competitive market mechanisms is scandalous.

The basic critique, then, proceeds from the curious *methodological* position that Kornai adopts:

> For the description of the economic system, mathematical economics has succeeded in constructing a formalized theoretical structure, *thus giving an impression of maturity*, but one of the main criteria of maturity, namely, verification, has hardly been satisfied. In comparison to the vast amount of work devoted to the construction of abstract theory, the amount of effort which has been applied, up to now, in checking the assumptions and statements seems inconsequential [p.17].

This argument, which expresses many economists' resistance to general equilibrium analysis, is usually not asserted with as much clarity and openness, and it is to Kornai's credit that he had both the courage and the intellectual strength to do more than just carp at the ADM model: his book attempted to rectify the perceived problems.

The critique however denies Lakatos' discussion of scientific progress, or what theories are supposed to achieve. It is also misleading as a statement about the role of general equilibrium theory itself. Our own use of "general equilibrium theory" forces the rejoinder to Kornai that:

(1) There has never been a reputable economist who claimed that the ADM system was a *descriptive* model.

(2) Since all assumptions are counterfactual ("assume the mass of the sphere is concentrated at the center," "assume electrons jump orbits according to quantum rules") it is unclear what could be meant by "checking the assumptions," presumably for verisimilitude.

(3) "Verification" is a will-o-the-wisp. Science does not proceed by verifying propositions derived from theory, although in some cases it may involve "falsification," rejecting partial theories for which the derived propositions may be disconfirmed.

(4) All empirical work in demand theory, say, is a test of the kind that Kornai wishes to have, since the implications of optimizing behavior are precisely the propositions that demand analysis exists and can be confronted with data.

(5) The general equilibrium theories that we shall examine in Part II, the modern program of neo-Walrasian analysis, have, as their implications, a variety of macroeconomic propositions. Tests of these are indirect tests of the theories that, at one remove, have generated them.

(6) All theories are not equal. In large measure, general equilibrium theory is the defining hard core, in Lakatos' sense, of the neo-Walrasian research program. What is tested, or empirically examined, are a large set of derived and interrelated propositions in the "protective belt" of the hard core. Most scientific work is carried out in the protective belt. The hard core, which for much of current economics is precisely general equilibrium theory, is only abandoned if the research program itself is both degenerative *and* replaceable by another more progressive program. Kornai's confusion on this matter is widely shared. Anyone who argues that "neo-classical economics will be non-sensical as long as rational economic agents are asssumed" is committing the same kind of methodological blunder. Scientific methodology is more than obeisance to the experimental method.

This is not to say that general equilibrium theory has no flaws. It has many. But the strength of the original ADM construction has been to guide economists to the weak points of the theory.

In any event, by the 1960s both static and dynamic ADM models began to proliferate into applied areas of economic theory, in international trade, public finance, and more to our concerns here, into monetary theory.

In Chapter 4 we shall explore the growing symbiosis between the neo-Walrasian program and elements of post-war monetary theory and macroeconomics. We shall then be in a better position to assess the current state of the literature on the microfoundations of macroeconomics. But first we must take a detour into the economics of Keynes, for macroeconomics was based on his analysis.

3

The 4,827th reexamination of Keynes' system

"The price we pay for anticipation of the future is anxiety about it. Foretelling disaster is probably not much fun; Polyanna was much happier than Cassandra. But the Cassandric components of our nature are necessary for survival. The doctrines for regulating the future that they produced are the origins of ethics, magic, science, and legal codes. The benefit of foreseeing catastrophe is the ability to take steps to avoid it, sacrificing short-term for long-term benefits" [Sagan, 1977, p. 71].

Current reinterpretations of the microfoundations of macroeconomics require examination of the structure of the macroeconomic theory that has emerged in the forty-plus years since Keynes "revolutionized" the discipline.

Unfortunately, there is today no accepted view of what it was that Keynes actually accomplished. There is no easy answer to the question of how standard macroeconomic analysis differs from Keynes' own vision. It would seem that we must tackle the problem which has occupied theorists for decades, of identifying the system of *Keynes* and tracing its transmogrification at the hands of both Keynesians and anti-Keynesians of innumerable persuasions. This herculean task might not, however, untangle current analytic problems.

For better or worse, questions about "what Keynes really meant" stand apart from the creation of rigorous, analytically tractable, and sufficiently rich microfoundations structures. We are interested in studying those "generalized" general equilibrium structures which generate macroeconomic insights. Consequently this chapter will set out various elements of the *General Theory* in a form which will motivate our discussion in Chapter 4 of the early microfoundations of macroeconomics literature of Hicks, Lange, Klein, and Patinkin.

In particular, we shall present two alternative interpretations of the basic Keynesian system, discuss their various components, and indicate the sorts of enquiries that flow from each when taken as a guide to research. We shall see that one of these interpretations, the standard income–expenditure model, is particularly well-suited to restatement in neo-Walrasian terms, so well-suited, in fact, that the alternative vision, which Coddington calls "Chapter 12 Keynesianism" represents a line of innovative analysis that dropped from sight as Keynes became a "Keynesian" through the years of the neo-Walrasian synthesis.

Keynes as a neo-Walrasian

Our purpose, in these few pages, is simply to document that it is not entirely outrageous, or intellectually reprehensible, to interpret *The General Theory of Employment, Interest, and Money* as a rudimentary neo-Walrasian system, or "income–expenditure model" (a là Leijonhufvud). It may not be correct to do so, but it is not a fraudulent exercise since it does have its genesis in Keynes's own writings.

As early as 1932, as Keynes was shaping the manuscript which was to develop later into the *General Theory*, we find his basic method of enquiry laid out in clear terms: "All the factors in a monetary economy which make up the total economic situation are in some degree interdependent, and react on one another. Let us, nevertheless, without implying that any one is either wholly independent of, or causally prior to, the others, endeavor to clear our minds by considering them one by one" [Keynes, Vol. 13, p. 397].

This is very Marshallian in tone, but the method itself is naturally suited to a general equilibrium treatment when the "factors" are considered simultaneously. That this cannot be too different from what Keynes sometimes had in mind may be seen from a 1934 draft of the *General Theory*, especially Chapter 9 of the draft called "The functions relating employment, consumption, and investment" [Keynes, Vol. 13, pp. 439–42].

In that chapter Keynes defines the propensity to consume (or consumption function) measured in wage units as

$$C_w = f_1 \ (N, \ r, \ E)$$

where N is amount of employment, r is the rate of interest, and E is the state of long-term expectations. Similarly, the propensity to invest is written as

$$I_w = f_2 \ (N, \ r, \ E)$$

On standard arguments, r and E are "suppressed" in f_1 and N is "suppressed" in f_2 to yield

$$C_w = f_1(N)$$

$$I_w = f_2(r, \ E)$$

Thus if aggregate demand is D_w, then

$$D_w = C_w + I_w$$

If this function is taken in conjunction with the employment function, related to aggregate supply, we have a goods market equilibrium condition to determine the volume of employment.

This argument is clearly spelled out in Chapter 3 of the *General Theory*. Briefly, the "volume of employment is given by the point of intersection between the aggregate demand function and the aggregate supply function" [Keynes, 1936, p. 25].

The functions are not quite the traditional schedules in price–quantity space, but rather a relationship in money income and employment space where "the aggregate supply price of the output of a given amount of employment is the expectation of

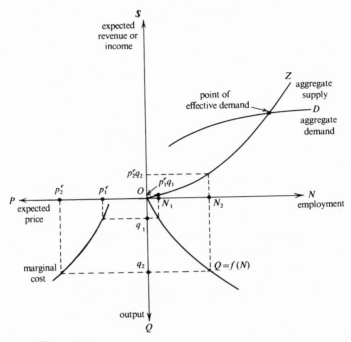

Figure 3.1

proceeds which will just make it worth the while of the entrepreneurs to give that employment" [p. 24]. Aggregate supply is thus a schedule relating levels of expected money income to levels of employment: given a price expectation, p^*, for a unit of output, there is, for a given technology and factor price (wage) structure, a profit maximizing output q. A microproduction function can relate this q to an employment level N. And the schedule of p^*q versus N is the aggregate supply function, denoted by Keynes as $(p^*q =)Z = \varphi(N)$. "Similarly, let D be the proceeds which entrepreneurs expect to receive from the employment of N men, the relationship between D and N being written $D = f(N)$, which can be called the *Aggregate Demand Function*" [p. 25]. The graphs of these schedules are given in Figure 3.1.

To understand the diagram, begin in the third quadrant. Pick an expected price p_1^e. Profit maximization under perfect competition generates, from the marginal cost (*MC*) schedule, a profit maximizing output q_1. In quadrant two, from the firm's production function, $Q = f(N)$, find the number of workers necessary to produce that output: call it N_1. The point $(N_1, p_1^e q_1)$ is on Z, the aggregate supply curve. Changing p_1^e to p_2^e gives another point, and so on.

For aggregate demand D, every employment total generates a stream of factor payments. These are realized income to the factors and they thus generate demand signals, in nominal terms, which are consistent with the original expectations of the firms.

Working, as Keynes did, in such highly aggregative fashion with the supply and demand for output as a whole, it is hardly surprising that everything of interest was tucked into the parameters of the schedules, their shapes and components, and their mutual interactions. For Keynes, the aggregate supply function was least troublesome for it merely extended the traditional supply concepts. For a single firm, the relation between expected proceeds and employment could be found by assuming no more than a marginal cost curve which, in p–q space, sloped upward and reflected diminishing returns. Since Keynes' units were money sums and employment sums, these schedules could be "added" to obtain the aggregate supply function.

On the demand side, however, Keynes noted that D was the sum of demands for consumption and investment, so these categories had to be separately analyzed. Book III (Chapters 8–10) was thus devoted to explicating the determinants of consumption demand, while the first two chapters (11 and 12) of Book IV initiated the discussion of the investment decision. The interest rate, playing a role in the investment function, needed further analysis and so Chapters 13–17 presented the theory of liquidity preference to anchor the interest rate, and thus investment and aggregate demand.

Book V returned to the aggregate supply function and presented the implications of changing money wages and prices on employment through changes in aggregate supply and demand.

To see how this structure was used by Keynes for analytic

purposes consider the arguments, presented in Chapter 19, about the efficacy of money wage reductions to combat unemployment. In the classical model, employment was determined (see Chap. 2, pp. 5–7 of the *General Theory*) by the intersection of the supply for labor and the (derived) demand for labor. Classical economists accepted the implicit argument that "a reduction in money-wages will, cet. par., stimulate demand by diminishing the price of the finished product, and will therefore increase output and employment up to the point where the reduction which labor has agreed to accept in its money wages is just offset by the diminishing marginal efficiency of labor as output (from a given equipment) is increased" [p. 257].

For Keynes [p. 258] this analysis is fundamentally wrong for it "is tantamount to assuming that the reduction in money-wages will leave demand unaffected," but the entire "question at issue is whether the reduction in money-wages will or will not be accompanied by the same aggregate effective demand as before measured in money" [p.259].

Keynes' analysis of this problem thus involved tracing the effects of a change in money wages on the aggregate demand schedule through its components the consumption function, investment function, and liquidity preference schedule. The argument presented [pp. 262–9 *GT*] showed that the reduction in money wages would first, through some price reductions, redistribute income away from workers and thus likely diminish consumption. Second, if the reduction "is expected to be a *reduction relatively to money wages in the future,* the change will be favourable to investment, because ... it will increase the marginal efficiency of capital." Finally, the reduction will reduce money incomes and thus "will diminish the need for cash for income and business purposes; and it will therefore reduce *pro tanto* the schedule of liquidity preference."

Only this last effect is unambiguous, since the others depended on delicate redistributive or expectations assumptions. "It is, therefore, on the effect of a falling wage- and price-level on the demand for money that those who believe in the self-adjusting quality of the economic system must rest the weight of their argument." Granting this, we "can, therefore, theoretically at least, produce precisely the same effects on the rate of interest by reducing wages, whilst leaving the quantity of money unchanged, that we can produce by increasing the quantity of money whilst leaving the level of wages unchanged."

We have presented this argument in some detail since it is not only an excellent example of how a Marshallian type argument "worked," but it is one which is a natural candidate for a more detailed treatment by means of interrelated markets, by neo-Walrasian methods. In its simplest terms, there are three markets involved: consumer goods, investment goods, and money. Treating the money wage and the quantity of money as parameters, the argument begins with a reduction in money wages. This reduces the level of money income for wage earners which appears as an argument of the demand functions for consumption, investment, and money.

Since the consumption function will be unaffected in the main (rentier income *increases* as worker income declines), and investment can only really be influenced by *expected* income levels, the demand for money will bear the brunt of the adjustment. If $M = L(Y, r)$ where M is the nominal quantity of money and Y is nominal income, fixed M and reduced Y entails a reduced rate of interest, which stimulates I since $\partial I/\partial r < 0$ and, via the multiplier, increases income. Money wage cuts then depend crucially, for their value in combating unemployment, on the interest rate sensitivity of both the demand for money and the demand for investment. This general equilibrium, or multimarket, formulation seems to express this particular argument rather well.

It should further be noted that this framework, akin to the early Hicks income–expenditure model of IS and LM schedules, received Keynes' *approval* in a letter to Hicks, [Collected works, Vol. 14, p. 79]. This analysis essentially suppressed *both* the bond market and the labor market, and studied only the interaction between the markets for goods and money.

What happens, however, when we attempt to add the labor

market to this system, as would appear natural within the neo-Walrasian program? As good Keynesians, our focus should naturally be upon the demand for labor and, to be consistent with Keynes' units of measurement, should involve only units of employment and money.

But it should be clear that employment itself is already determined in Keynes' system, since the intersection of aggregate supply and demand occurs in income–employment space. Consequently, the "labor market" is redundant once goods and money markets are present. Put another way, the only legitimate way to model "employment" as being determined in a labor market is to embed the goods and money markets in the schedules that go to make up the supply and demand functions in that labor market. This is not too difficult to accomplish, of course, and in fact constitutes Chapter 20 of the *General Theory*, "The Employment Function." Briefly, since the aggregate supply curve was originally drawn under assumptions of fixed factor prices (i.e., wages) we can change the level of money wages and trace out the resulting employment totals from the points of effective demand. That is, for w_1, find N_1, the intersection of aggregate supply, Z_1, and demand, D_1. Repeat for w_2, Z_2, D_2 and the resulting N_2. Relating the wages and employments in a schedule, we have the employment function that Keynes described. This is done in Figs 3.2a and b.

In Fig. 3.2a N_1 workers are employed at wages w_1. If wages increase to w_2, the new aggregate supply and demand curves give a point of effective demand with N_2 workers employed. The graph of (N, w), in Fig. 3.2b, is the employment function. It is, however, fundamentally an equilibrium relationship, or profile of employment equilibria for different money wage levels. What it most assuredly is *not* is an aggregate demand curve for labor in any usual sense. But in order to work any variant of the neo-Walrasian argument, it is necessary to treat all markets, including the labor market, in a symmetric fashion. Just as supply and demand determined goods and money balance totals, so too should supply and demand for labor determine employment totals. The natural

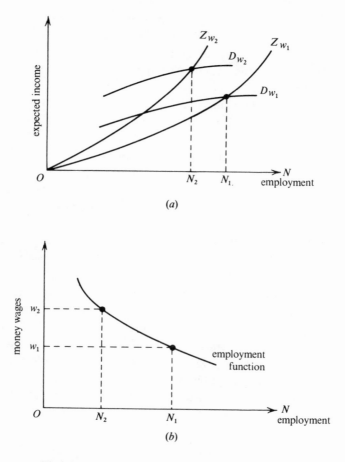

Figure 3.2

bias in neo-Walrasian reasoning is to *first* set out all the various market equilibrium relationships, then drop one via Walras' Law type reasoning. For the Keynesian system clearly the labor market must go in the sense that the demand curve for labor is *not* given by any aggregate marginal productivity relationship.

This aggregate supply–aggregate demand model, which is clearly based on the *General Theory*, is not the usual income–expenditure system of American textbooks. Since it is easily translated into the four-quadrant *IS–LM* structure [Roberts, 1975] with the addition of money and employment markets and assumptions about the distributional changes of changing employment totals, we shall continue to refer to either the *Z–D* or *IS–LM* constructions as income–expenditure Keynesian models. The *Z–D* emphasizes (1) expectations by firms of the prices at which finished output can be sold and (2) employment as a result of those short-run expectations. This makes the *Z–D* model somewhat more useful as a device for comparing the treatment of price expectations in general equilibrium theory with their treatment in Keynes' work. The *Z–D* model was developed by S. Weintraub [1958] and extended by Davidson and Smolensky [1962] and Davidson [1972].

In any event, it should be apparent that an income–expenditure version of Keynes' analysis does not entirely miss the point of the *General Theory*. Further, a neo-Walrasian reconstruction is not a completely inappropriate framework for discussing the systemic interactions in the Keynesian model. What is somewhat unsettling, however, is that the neo-Walrasian bias towards a symmetric treatment of all markets may obscure the economics of their linkages if the symmetry is pursued at the expense of economic analysis. We shall see in the next chapter just how the requisite self-policing within the neo-Walrasian program worked in fact.

Even with full awareness of such difficulties a number of elements of Keynes' analysis could *not* be treated in the neo-Walrasian model. It is to such matters that we now must turn, for if these elements were crucial to Keynes' theory, the neo-Walrasian reconstruction of Keynes, the synthesis that took so long to develop, is logically flawed and produces semantic confusion when it is termed "Keynesian economics."

"Chapter 12 Keynesianism"[1]

There is an alternative view of Keynes' system which has

---

[1] Portions of this section are drawn from [E. R. Weintraub, 1975b]. Permission to reprint is by courtesy of the Duke University Press. The title of this section is due to Coddington [1976].

recently been associated with Post-Keynesians like Joan Robinson, Kaldor, Shackle, Davidson, Minsky, Kregel, Coddington, S. Weintraub, Harcourt, et al. This takes, as one point of departure, certain themes introduced in Chapter 12 of the *General Theory* (on "The State of Long Term Expectations") already presaged in the *Treatise on Money*, and which ended in the 1937 *Quarterly Journal of Economics* article "The General Theory of Employment."

A bit of history and biography might help put some later matters in perspective: "Between 1906 and 1911 Keynes was devoting all his spare time to the theory of Probability . . . In 1912 other work supervened, and his treatise had to be left on one side until 1920, when he polished it up before its appearance in 1921. Thus it was his work from the age of twenty-three to twenty-nine" [Harrod, 1966, p. 133]. This work attempted to carry out, for the theory of probability, the program initiated by Russell and Whitehead for mathematics, namely, to provide a logical foundation for the subject. At that time the only explicit theory which delineated the meaning of the proposition "the probability that x is y is p" was that of Venn, which provided a relative frequency interpretation of probability statements. Such a theory asserted that the meaning of "the probability that x is y is p" was that a large number of cases had been examined in which x was y and x was not y, and p was the proportion of the former in the total number of cases.

For Keynes, however, probability language was also applied to real choice situations beyond the casino. In assessing alternative plans for action, men are guided by their views of the most likely outcome. But outcomes are in the future and are not observed today. "The probability is 0.50 that it will rain tomorrow" is not a statement about worlds of possible tomorrows in half of which rain occurs, but rather an expression of our confidence in the fact that tomorrows are like yesterdays. More telling, however, is the observation that experiments like those with a roulette wheel are unavailable; we cannot get more knowledge of the future until it is here, but the decision whether to go to the beach tomorrow must be made today.

In Chapter 8 of *A Treatise on Probability* [1973 edition], Keynes rejected the relative frequency theory, since "if we allow it to hold the field, we must admit that probability is not the guide to life, and in following it we are not acting according to reason" [p. 104]. Instead, Keynes suggested that probability was related, not to the balance between favorable and unfavorable evidence, but to the balance "between the absolute amounts of relevant knowledge and of relevant ignorance ... an accession of new evidence increases the weight of an argument. New evidence will sometimes decrease the probability of an argument, but will always increase its 'weight' " [p. 77].

Keynes' argument was that to use probability to guide choice in matters of fundamental uncertainty one needed to discuss not only probability but also the confidence one held in that probability. A high probability does not entail more certainty than a low one, since uncertainty is primarily characterized by a lack of confidence in probability as "a guide to life." Consequently an economic agent ought not to maximize expected payoffs, when each of an array of payoffs is assigned a probability number by the agent, if he has little confidence in those probabilities.

In modern parlance, it was Keynes' view that a major leap of faith is involved in treating situations characterized by uncertainty as situations involving only risk. Any choice now among future alternatives is fundamentally uncertain, since the future is logically unknowable. No sampling from the future is feasible to ascertain probabilities for future alternatives, so there is no philosophically sound way by which uncertainty problems can be reduced to problems involving risk.

Let us now jump in time to 1937. The *General Theory* had appeared the previous year, critics had begun to respond, and Keynes could deal with the central theme directly since his more detailed arguments had been presented:

> I sum up therefore, the main grounds for my departure [from the traditional theory] as follows: (1) the orthodox theory assumes that we have a knowledge of the future of a kind quite different from that which we actually possess.

> This false rationalisation follows the lines of the
> Benthamite calculus. The hypothesis of a calculable future
> leads to a wrong interpretation of the principles of
> behavior which the need for action compels us to adopt,
> and to an under-estimation of the concealed factors of
> utter doubt, precariousness, hope and fear [Volume 14,
> p. 121].

Keynes here argued that in traditional theory situations involving uncertainty had been handled by probability tools appropriate
for dealing with risk. Traditional theory assumed that one could
maximize expected payoffs, even though expected values could
not be confidently calculated. And yet individuals must act today;
the effects of their choices will only be known in the future, but all
economic activity undertaken at one time has intertemporal
consequences. Economic man then must base decisions on something; that something is (1) the recent past and (2) what others are
doing, but such a choice framework, "being based on so flimsy a
foundation . . . is subject to sudden and violent changes" [Volume
14, p. 114].

What relationship does this theme of the uncertainty matrix of
economic decisions bear to the central theme of the *General
Theory*? To answer this, we need to consider just what Keynes felt
he had done that was important:

> My theory can be summed up by saying that, given the
> psychology of the public, the level of output and
> employment as a whole depends on the amount of
> investment . . . [Although some other factors can affect
> output] it is those which determine the rate of investment
> which are more unreliable, since it is they which are
> influenced by our views of the future about which we
> know so little [Volume 14, p. 121].

In other words, employment depended on the level of output,
and the level of output depended on the level of investment. In a
formal sense investment, as the marginal efficiency of capital
schedule, was the discounted value of the income the capital asset
was expected to generate over its life; the discount factor was the

interest rate on bonds, a "long" rate. Bonds and capital goods were perfect substitutes on the "long" end of the spectrum of asset-lives. Since, however, bond prices (and thus interest rates) were primarily determined by speculative bullishness and bearishness in the market, expected earnings determined investment, and such long-term expectations could not be analyzed by standard choice theory, since the earnings stream stretched well into the very uncertain future.

To this argument, the traditional economist would raise several objections. (1) The employment level so determined must be full employment, since an excess supply of workers at a wage would force wages down, thus bringing about full employment at a lower wage; (2) even if an expectations collapse led to a decline in the quantity of investment, the supply of loanable funds (from savings which depend directly on the interest rate) would then exceed the demand (for investment purposes), so the excess supply would force the interest rate back down to equilibrium level.

Either of these two arguments (or both) were somewhat characteristic of the doctrines Keynes attacked. They each support the view of a capitalist market economy as a stable system; the price mechanism, in the various markets, would damp down deviations from equilibrium. The economy was viewed as self-regulated, so, if unemployment existed, it must have been caused by rigidities or obstructions to the natural working of the market mechanism.

Keynes denied both arguments. On wage reduction he contended that someone in the labor market, buyers and sellers of labor services, had to lower real wages and both had control of money wages only. Although a decline in money wages might lower money prices and thus stimulate demand for goods and thus employment, money wages were income to wage earners and their demand for goods would fall. Little could be expected from money wage cuts in a world of unemployment. On interest rates, Keynes denied that the volume of savings depended on the rate of interest to any real extent. Decisions to invest generated income that was spent, or saved. Expenditures on non-consumer-goods had to equal income received but not spent on consumer goods, so measured savings always equaled measured investment.

Consequently, uncertainty (as it impinged primarily on the investment decision) was the culprit in involuntary unemployment. A collapse in expectations could lead to a fall in investment which, via the multiplier, could amplify the initial disturbance to reduce output and employment. Full employment was more a characteristic of Heaven , where the future could never bring surprise; on this planet, where business plans for an unknown tomorrow by taking action today, unemployment is not unlikely.

One final point should be noted. The facts (1) that capital assets are long-lived, (2) that a desire to hold money is a measure of our distrust of the future, and (3) that production takes time, are all facts which pertain to a world in which time is essential. We have seen how time and uncertainty were intermingled; the existence of the former necessarily entailed the latter. Keynes' system was dynamic in the traditional sense of involving time in an essential manner. If investment is volatile, because of uncertainty, no one level of output or employment might ever be maintained. It is in this sense that uncertainty can be called a disequilibrium phenomenon, and Keynes can be said to have dealt with disequilibrium problems. At any rate, it should be clear that adjustments to an equilibrium level of employment are meaningless in a world of uncertainty, for there might be no equilibrium in the sense of a maintained state of the system.

As an example of how Keynes' views have been extended, by Post-Keynesian theorists, let us examine a recent critique of general equilibrium theory, from the microfoundations of macroeconomics viewpoint, which appears in Paul Davidson's "Money and General Equilibrium" [1977]. Davidson, a leading Post-Keynesian and lucid analyst of the monetary theoretic framework of Keynes' work, attacks general equilibrium (GE) theory in a variety of ways. He argues that, in the Theory " it is normally believed that the simultaneous clearing of *all* markets is a necessary and sufficient condition for GE" [p. 7]. Further,

> The intellectual auxiliary baggage of gross substitution,
> Walras' Law, Say's Principle, optimality of reconciled

choices of all agents via the price system, etc. are so closely identified with the concept of general equilibrium, while this paraphernalia is so incompatible with a monetary economy, that to apply the term GE to a monetary equilibrium system would seem to me to be a semantic travesty [p. 25].

Although Davidson's analysis confuses the idea of "equilibrium" in a general system with the notion of a "competitive equilibrium" in an ADM model, the basic problem here is that general equilibrium theory is identified with a *specific model*, and the theory is denied meaning on the grounds that a twenty year old model (Patinkin's) in the GE tradition has some major inadequacies when used to examine a variety of questions in monetary theory. Davidson explicitly denies that the referent of the term general equilibrium theory could be a set of models with mutually contradictory assumptions and induced propositions.

Post-Keynesian arguments of this type are perhaps applicable to early work in general equilibrium theory. Indeed, the task of Part II will be to show how recent work has attempted to rekindle interest in "Chapter 12" Keynesianism and to provide a set of sophisticated models capable to dealing, in an integrated fashion, with the variety of insights and innovations that Keynes introduced when "macroeconomics" was created.

We must first understand how income–expenditure systems were linked to neo-Walrasian analysis, for this synthesis is the substance of the "standard" microfoundations of macroeconomics. Later developments are built on these models; their defects are the guiding force for much current work.

What comes next

The foregoing suggests that it is easy to draw various lessons from Keynes' canon. This is a stumbling block of sorts for a rational reconstruction of the microfoundations for Keynes' analysis, although such investigations and interpretations have shaped much of modern theory. In order to bring our story up to 1960, then, we shall investigate, in the next chapter, how the neo-Walrasian research program shaped the content of Keynesian-ism and document how the "neo-classical counterrevolution" (as Clower terms it) came into being. Our method will be to examine the contributions of Hicks, Lange, Klein, and Patinkin and to see the emerging neo-Walrasian interpretations of Keynes' work, at least that part of his work which could be reduced to income–expenditure analysis.

4

The neo-Walrasian synthesis[1]

J. R. Hicks' *Value and Capital*, published in 1939, is rightly considered a classic in economics for its rigorous treatment of household and firm behavior under competitive conditions. What is less frequently appreciated today is that it was an attempt to lay the conceptual groundwork for macroeconomics in a well-specified Walrasian system.

> I believe I have had the fortune to come upon a method of analysis which is applicable to a wide variety of economics problems . . . it is, perhaps, most illuminating when it is applied to the most complex problems (such as those of trade fluctuations) . . . The method of General Equilibrium, which these writers [Walras, Pareto, and Wicksell] elaborated, was especially designed to exhibit the economic system as a whole, in the form of a complex pattern of interrelations of markets . . . When we come to dynamic problems, I shall not neglect to pay attention to the important work which has been done in that field by Marshallian methods—I allude in particular to the work of Mr. Keynes . . . [with our methods] we shall thus be able to see just why it is that Mr. Keynes reaches different results from earlier economists on crucial matters of social policy [pp. 1–5].

[1] A modified version of this chapter appears as [E. R. Weintraub, 1977].

The structure of *Value and Capital* itself reflects Hicks' absorption with microfoundations topics. Initial chapters present the theory of consumer behavior and general equilibrium of exchange. Production is introduced and competitive equilibrium is "established" and, in Part III, the concept of "temporary equilibrium" makes its appearance. This equilibrium is over a Hicksian week and represents the adjustment of demands and productions to a set of price expectations held on a "Monday." With those expectations, outputs and inputs are determined and markets work to equilibrate supply and demand. Some individuals may find that their expectations are falsified by the market activity over the week, but it is not until the following "Monday" that expectations may be revised in light of last week's results to set consumption and production plans for week number two.

Temporary equilibrium is different from the ADM competitive equilibrium in the sense that it involves expectations. By construction there are insufficient presently existing futures markets to establish a simultaneous current market prereconciliation of multi-period plans *and* expectations.

Temporary equilibrium consequently focuses attention on those markets where the future impinges on this week's decisions. In this monetized system money, financial claims, and capital goods provide the intertemporal linkage. The Hicksian framework thus embodies the Keynesian concern that a money–production economy is intertwined with expectations phenomena, so that in a world of perfect certainty few Keynesian insights are relevant.

As Hicks correctly noted,

> So long as economists were content to regard the economic system in static fashion, it was reasonable to treat it as a self-righting mechanism . . . As soon as we take expectations into account (or rather, as soon as we take the elasticity of expectations into account), the stability of the system is seriously weakened . . . It is henceforth not at all surprising that the economic system of reality should be subject to large fluctuations, nor that these fluctuations should be so very dangerous [p. 256].

If equilibrium is to be "stable," each period's temporary equilibrium should "match up" in a coherent fashion so that all markets work to reconcile choices made by the various economic units. The absence of futures markets precludes any once-and-for-all pre-reconciliation. Instead money, capital goods, and financial assets are the only intertemporal link since, for example, a decision to hold money in week one provides income which can be spent in week two. The mechanism which determines the intertemporal structure of decisions is expectational in nature. Price expectations depend, however, on past and current prices and consequently any change in prices generates a change in price expectations and thus a change in the temporary equilibrium. Successive changes either "settle down" over time or they don't, depending on the properties "of money and of securities, those awkward things which are not demanded for their own sake, but as means to the purchase of commodities at future dates" [p. 259].

Analysis of macroeconomic arguments was carried out by Hicks using this temporary equilibrium framework. For example, if prices fall from some exogenous shock, expectations are affected and it is necessary on some assumptions for the rate of interest to fall to restore equilibrium. If unemployment is a systemic failure, then perhaps *barriers* to the fall in the rate of interest are a culprit in depressions [p. 259].

The logic of Hicks' extended Walrasian system provided a method for evaluating macroeconomic propositions. If aggregate structures fail to provide a resolution of controversy, then a disaggregated neo-Walrasian system could perhaps provide sufficient detail to clarify complicated lines of argument. In Hicks' hands, the tools seemed so easy to manipulate. The theory is clear in its presuppositions and direct in its implications.

Despite these words of tribute, there were some flaws in Hicks' analysis. His reach extended his grasp through no fault of intellectual integrity but because of some subtle mathematical issues not even posed at the time *Value and Capital* was written.

As noted in Chapter 2, issues surrounding the existence of equilibrium were not treated prior to the Arrow–Debreu paper with the exception of the somewhat unaccessible series of papers by Wald. The *existence* of a temporary equilibrium could not really be discussed without a formalization of competitive equilibrium proper, and hence the role of money emerged as a problem for the general equilibrium framework.

More importantly, the weight of Hicks' arguments about the dynamics of the Keynesian system presupposed a coherent stability theory for the temporary equilibrium, *a fortiori* for the competitive equilibrium. But Hicks, despite his presentation of "perfect" and "imperfect" stability ideas, was simply wrong in his analysis. It was not until Samuelson's work that stability theory was properly set down, and theorems about stability of a competitive economy were not established until the late 1950s (see Chapter 2).

As a consequence, Hicks' propositions were both stronger and weaker then they appeared. They were stronger in the sense that if Hicks' assumptions entailed existence and stability of a temporary equilibrium, then Hicks' macroeconomic implications were secure and there was simply no issue at all about the microfoundations of macroeconomics. *Value and Capital* would be weaker, though, to the extent that later theorists found that assumptions necessary to ensure existence and stability did violence to the integrity of the Hicks structure.

As a consequence of this dilemma, work based on *Value and Capital* was concerned not so much with the macroeconomic implications of the general equilibrium approach, but with the logical coherence of that general equilibrium system itself. It was not as if macroeconomists repudiated Hicks' assistance, but rather that questions of (*a*) proper modelling of a monetary general equilibrium system, (*b*) existence, and (*c*) stability were more problematical than Hicks had suggested.

Despite this fact, perusal of the post-Hicksian literature, particularly modern work on temporary equilibrium, suggests that Hicks was thirty years too early for the economics profession. To this day there have been few works so grand in conception or so pregnant with new ideas about the basic structure of economic theory. The microfoundations of macroeconomic theory that Hicks identified helped to create the neo-Walrasian revolution that has survived to

this day. The structure of individual choice, the market interrelationships, the sophistication of the various asset market specifications, the treatment of expectations, money wages, contracts (spot
and forward), and prices provided economists with a comprehensive vision of both microeconomics and Keynesian macroeconomics. The identification of "temporary equilibrium" alone was an
intellectual triumph of the first order.

Microfoundations works subsequent to *Value and Capital,* like
Lange's and Patinkin's to be examined shortly, are drawn on but a
portion of Hicks' canvas. They had to go deeper into the
pecularities of modelling a monetized economy, for Hicks never
quite tied his numeraire to money. They had to be clearer about
equilibrium and stability, for Hicks had not the benefit of modern
mathematics. But as a consequence, the grand Hicksian conception was progressively limited, and "temporary equilibrium"
thinking was reduced to competitive equilibrium about which
propositions could be more readily established. With the microeconomic structure thus limited, the induced macroeconomic
models became less "Keynesian" and more "classical." The
neo-Walrasian revolution as it developed was indeed initiated by
Hicks' *Value and Capital*, but its direction was determined by that
book's weaknesses on some of the formal problems and not by the
book's strength of imagination and insight. As shall be seen in Part
II, it has taken over thirty years to reintroduce the temporary
equilibrium concept into the neo-Walrasian program.

Oscar Lange

Lange's *Price Flexibility and Employment* appeared in
1944 and attempted to incorporate the formal dynamic stability
theory introduced by Samuelson into the Hicksian general equilibrium structure in order to evaluate Keynesian theory.

By focusing his attention on the substitution of money for goods,
Lange analyzed the effect of factor price changes on commodity
and factor prices. This concern was expressly linked to Keynes
since Lange appeared to accept the argument that, in a classical
model, unemployment (an excess supply of labor) would be

eliminated by flexibility of money wages. His arguments were constructed to show how, in a general equilibrium model, factor price flexibility might induce multimarket repercussions which would not ameliorate the involuntary unemployment.

Lange introduced the notion of a "monetary" effect which is the general reaction to a proportional change in all prices (the price level). A "positive monetary effect," for example, is present when individuals substitute goods for money when the price level falls, and it can be established that, with such an effect, a fall in the price of an unemployed factor reduces its excess supply.

The questions of interest thus reduce to the interaction of money and goods or, more precisely, the way in which money enters into the real (goods) equations of an appropriately specified general equilibrium system. The intuitive notion of a dichotomy between the determination of relative prices and absolute prices of course precludes a positive monetary effect. If excess demand functions for goods are homogeneous of degree zero in all prices, then a proportionate fall in all prices leaves excess demands unchanged.

Such an analysis treats money and goods symmetrically. It leaves the determination of the absolute price level outside the system. This can be seen in another way: since a fixed nominal money supply always induces a positive monetary effect, on quantity theory reasoning the absolute price level is thus pegged.

Keynesian concerns are introduced via Hicksian expectations. The possibility of intertemporal substitution requires that the monetary system change the nominal quantity of money as the real demand for cash balances changes. Positive monetary effects (which, recall, eliminate unemployment) thus require a responsive monetary system under conditions of elastic price expectations.

With real price uncertainty, when "the real quantity of money is held constant, the monetary effect . . . may be rather weak . . . [so] greater fluctuations of prices are required to secure automatic maintenance or restoration of equilibrium in the markets of factors of production through flexibility of their prices" [p. 34].

Lange thus showed that some Keynesian arguments could be

well-posed in a general equilibrium model. This neo-Walrasian system was more rigorously specified than Hicks', and exploited Samuelson's stability analysis. The cost of such a specification was a loss in richness from *Value and Capital* even in the microeconomics. The temporary equilibrium concept was abandoned in favor of a competitive equilibrium of clearing all current markets, with all financial markets existing simultaneously with all goods markets.

The induced macromodel was more sterile as well. Macroeconomic questions were reduced to a single query: can factor price flexibility restore full employment, where full employment was identified with the competitive equilibrium? The story that Lange told was one of weaknesses in the multimarket interactions that precluded equilibrium outcomes.

Price Flexibility and Employment provides an early example of how the complex and interrelated macroeconomic insights of Keynes were lost as neo-Walrasian models were used to provide a microfoundations for all macroeconomics.

Lawrence R. Klein

Klein's *The Keynesian Revolution* (first edition) appeared in 1947 and was widely accepted as a survey of classical versus Keynesian theory. Although the focus of the book is macroeconomics, and *not* microfoundations, there is an implicit general equilibrium structure to the reasoning. This was developed in the technical appendix, particularly the section called "Mathematical Derivation of the System of *The General Theory*" [pp. 258–65].

The household has a utility function whose arguments are commodities and *future* commodities, securities and *future* securities, and cash balances at all dates. There is a period by period budget constraint which induces, by optimization, demand equations for both commodity flows and stocks of liquid assets for each period. *If the future is anticipated, and those anticipations are based on the past*, we have a system of market demand equations which are independent of the time period under a "suitable" aggregation scheme.

The production sector can be constructed by entrepreneurs' maximizing the present value of anticipated profits.

The resulting neo-Walrasian general equilibrium system, upon aggregation, induces a macroeconomic model which, Klein argues, can generate *either* classical *or* Keynesian conclusions depending on the shape (elasticities) of certain resulting functions.

Without laboring the point, Keynesian models were, to Klein, *not* characterized by rigidities: "In order to show that full employment is not automatic in a perfect world subject to Keynesian conditions, it is necessary to assume nothing whatsoever about rigidities in the system, but only to make plausible assumptions about the interest-inelasticity of certain basic relationships" [p. 89].

The microfoundations story, the neo-Walrasian structure, is well embedded in this argument. If time indeed is inessential, if money and financial assets have no true intertemporal roles, if production can be considered instantaneous, it is hardly surprising that the only difference between Keynesian and classical models is the empirically determinable size of certain parameters of aggregate functions. Keynesian models are *analytically* symmetric with classical models. They are *both* induced from neo-Walrasian systems and, although neither is *theoretically* preferable, Keynesian models pass muster on empirical grounds.

In retrospect, it is astounding how quickly the neo-Walrasian general equilibrium system was (a) stripped of its complexity and (b) assumed in its simple form to be compatible with macroeconomic concerns. The culmination of this process came with Patinkin's work which we must now examine, for *Money, Interest, and Prices* represented the final stage in the assimilation of Keynesian economics to the neo-Walrasian program.

Don Patinkin

In its scope, method, and scholarly craft, *Money, Interest, and Prices* is an intellectual tour de force. That it completed the neo-Walrasian structure in an analytically rigorous manner is by now well-understood. Its insight into Keynesian "disequilibrium" theory, however, was not so well-appreciated until Clower and Leijonhufvud began their "rehabilitation" of Keynes later in the 1960s (see Chapter 5).

Patinkin had two main analytic tasks:

(1) to examine the microeconomic decision structure in sufficient detail so that monetary theory would be anchored in a well-established choice-theoretic framework; and

(2) to "aggregate up," or to induce macroeconomic models which, by alternative macroeconomic specifications, could be identified as classical or Keynesian.

The major theme was "the monetary theory of an economy with full employment." Involuntary unemployment was treated as a second theme for monetary theory. Patinkin's Introduction announced the primary findings:

> The propositions of the quantity theory of money hold
> under conditions much less restrictive than those usually
> considered necessary by its advocates and, a fortiori, its
> critics. Conversely, the propositions of Keynesian
> monetary theory are much less general than the *General
> Theory* and later expositions would lead us to believe. But
> this in no way diminishes the relevance of Keynesian
> unemployment theory for the formulation of a practicable
> full-employment policy [p. xxv].

The book, subtitled "An Integration of Monetary Theory and Value Theory," is in two parts. I Microeconomics, and II Macroeconomics. The task of Part I was to "redo" Hicks' *Value and Capital* with money treated properly as a very special good, and *not* just as a numeraire in the general equilibrium system.

If we can caricature classical analysis by a model in which n excess demand equations determined $n-1$ *relative* prices while the equation of exchange determined the absolute price level, it is clear that monetary theory is impossible. The value of money or the reciprocal of the price level is supposed to be "given" by the equation of exchange in full employment. It is *also* supposed to be determined in the nth market and thus, by Walras' Law, in the $n-1$ goods markets. Thus the excess demand for money seems to be homogeneous of degree zero in prices from the "real" equations, but from the equation of exchange interpreted as an excess demand equation we have that excess demand is homogeneous of degree one in prices and the quantity of money. Thus the dichotomization of goods and money "sectors" is logically inconsistent.

What Patinkin did was to recognize clearly in his microeconomic analysis that the excess demand functions for commodities were the result of utility maximization subject to budget constraints, and that, in a monetary economy in which only money buys goods, households enter each period not only with income from sale of services (say), but also with cash balances carried over from the previous period. Put another way, in each period the household must decide not only how many commodities to purchase but the amount of cash balances to carry forward.

Consequently the budget constraint in each period will be of the form: the value of goods demanded plus the value of cash balances to be carried forward cannot exceed the value of goods supplied plus the value of cash balances held. The resulting excess demand functions for goods thus involve the household's intraperiod supply of real money balances as an argument. The excess demand function for real cash balances is treated symmetrically. Money has thus been integrated into the "real" general equilibrium system in an essential fashion, and all excess demand equations are homogeneous of degree zero in prices and the nominal quantity of money.

In concrete terms, a change in the nominal quantity of money will, as with Lange's work, entail a goods–money substitution and the effect, dubbed the "real-balance effect," will ramify throughout the entire general equilibrium structure. The substitutability is a systemic stabilizer (see Chapter 2), and the new equilibrium position will be characterized by an equiproportionate change in the price level. We see that Patinkin's system entails two classic quantity theory results: (*a*) the long run neutrality of monetary changes and (*b*) the influence of money supply variations on the price level. The equation of exchange, however, plays no role; its function is subsumed by a sophisticated treatment of the excess demand for real money balances.

Monetary theory without interest bearing assets is a travesty, so bonds are quickly integrated into Patinkin's analysis. Income streams involving payments in money generate an interest rate, so the excess demand function for bonds may be analyzed together with the excess demands for goods and money. From Walras' Law, leaving the labor market out is legitimate in equilibrium. The interest rate now appears properly as an argument of the various excess demand functions.

Patinkin's existence of equilibrium analysis is, to a mathematical reader, extremely curious. His procedure is to begin by counting equations and unknowns to see that they match up. Next, he imitates the heuristic of fixed point analysis in a surprising fashion. That is, each market is furnished with a tatonnement mechanism. An arbitrary price vector is posited, and the mechanism maps initial prices p^0 to p^1 via the excess demand function. p^1 is then mapped to p^2 and the process is conceived of as continuing through these "successive approximations." Recall that the structure of modern proofs is to construct a mapping, via the excess demand correspondence, and to show that it has as the desired equilibrium a fixed-point. Patinkin does not in fact carry out such a proof, but rather suggests that substitutability via the real balance effect will ensure that the successive p^i vectors will converge. In general, this procedure is not the problematic part of a modern existence proof. Rather, investigating the structure of the sets of prices themselves, on which the correspondence is defined, is an extremely delicate mathematical exercise. Nothing in Patinkin's analysis ensures, for example, that the equilibrium price of money is not zero.

This criticism is not meant to suggest that Patinkin's model is vacuous, for it is not. Rather, it forces awareness of some incompleteness of the general equilibrium analysis of *Money, Interest, and Prices*. The lacunae generated a great deal of work in the 1960s and 1970s, work which we shall examine in Part II.

The macroeconomic structure induced by the neo-Walrasian general equilibrium system is

        an aggregative model which divides all the goods of an

> economy into four composite categories: labor services, commodities, bonds, and money. To each of these categories there corresponds a market, a price, an aggregate demand function, and an aggregate supply function. Conceptually, each of these functions is built up from the individual demand and supply functions of the relevant individual goods . . . There is, however, no pretense of showing how this process of aggregation is actually carried out [pp. 199–200].

The labor market is given by a derived demand curve using marginal productivity which, under competition, is the real wage. Labor supply too depends on the real wage. Their intersection yields, in macro terms, full employment. In micro terms, it is a feature of the competitive equilibrium. For Patinkin, however, "The labor market as such does not interest us in the following analysis; its sole function is to provide the benchmark of full employment" [p. 205].

The analysis proceeds to show that, even with the presence of money and bonds in the model, and even with "Keynesian" specifications of the consumption function and liquidity preference, the qualitative properties of the system assure that the competitive equilibrium exists and is stable. Put another way, full employment outcomes are guaranteed by the specification of the model. *Keynes' concern to analyze the workings of an economy which had unemployment has been turned, in the neo-Walrasian program, into attempts to explain why the economic system should ever report unemployment at all.*

If Keynesian economics has any unique distinction, it must be in the area of policy, for it certainly takes no great wit or wisdom to "explain" unemployment in the neo-Walrasian system. Explanations of unemployment coincide with market failures, with logical barriers to the prereconciliation implicit in the competitive equilibrium position. Price rigidities in *any* market could induce unemployment. Further, the rigidities need not even be the classical ones like labor union intransigence, or money illusion. They may be market institutional data as suggested by Klein's "inelasticities."

Patinkin rejects such simple explanations for involuntary unemployment in Keynes' sense, although it is still a market failure argument that must be invoked since the competitive equilibrium is used as a reference point. In the system of *Money, Interest and Prices,* "belief in the efficacy of this monetary policy [open market operations] . . . will be identified here with the neoclassical position. Correspondingly, it is the denial of this efficacy which will be identified with the Keynesian one" [p. 336].

The Keynesian analysis, on Patinkin's view, holds two phenomena as primary: distribution effects and the influence of expectations. Both of these attributes of real economies are defined away in neo-Walrasian systems. Their only role is that of a destabilizer. "Thus Keynesian economics is the economics of unemployment disequilibrium. It argues that as a result of interest-inelasticity, on the one hand, and distribution and expectation effects, on the other, the dynamic process . . . even when aided by monetary policy . . . is unlikely to converge either smoothly or rapidly to the full-employment equilibrium position" [pp. 337–8].

Patinkin's Keynes did not deny, could not deny, the existence of a full-employment equilibrium, but rather was concerned to show that the equilibrium could not be readily attained. This analysis clearly shows that Keynes was *not* concerned with wage rigidities or similar institutional persiflage. On the other hand, accepting the Patinkin argument forces the view that Keynes could *not* have been saying anything of particular importance in theoretical terms. The emergent conclusion was that as a practical economist Keynes was undoubtedly correct in his diagnosis of disequilibrium and the need for intervention in markets by governments to stimulate demand.

Conclusion

From Hicks, through Lange and Klein, to Patinkin, we have seen a growing agreement about the particular microeconomic structure that is supposed to underlie all intelligent discourse about macroeconomic theory. This neo-Walrasian model is a certainty-based general equilibrium framework which includes various financial assets to store purchasing power over time. The assumptions of this model conform closely to that of the Arrow–Debreu–McKenzie (ADM) model discussed earlier, and the questions of existence, uniqueness, and stability of equilibrium can be examined under various assumptions.

The neo-Walrasian program proceeds from the positive heuristic which asserts that all economic phenomenon are reducible to statements about equilibrium positions of competitive systems. Obviously inefficient outcomes, like those involving involuntary unemployment, are always discussed as though they represent a systemic failure to reach the equilibrium. This point of view is absolutist in the extreme. No relativism of comparison between two actual positions of the economy can be allowed. Each position is studied with reference to the competitive equilibrium as "benchmark."

Comparing outcomes with the competitive equilibrium means that the language of the neo-Walrasian model structures the analysis of deviant positions. Whether this is a "good thing" or not is irrelevant: it is a fact which is not questioned within the neo-Walrasian frame of reference. The only apposite question is whether the program is a progressive one: whether (a) it continues to explain novel facts and (b) it continues to generate testable hypotheses.

As we shall see in Part II, there is much life left in the neo-Walrasian schema, especially since it has returned to Hicks' concept of "temporary equilibrium." Alternatives to the neo-Walrasian program are, at present, nowhere near as complex, fruitful, and robust. The neo-Walrasian synthesis of microeconomics and macroeconomics, for all its defects, remains a serious object for study.

5

General systemic coordination

What constitutes an "appropriate" microfoundation for macro-economics has been answered, implicitly, by most economists brought up in the neo-Walrasian tradition. If any single point of view can be said to have prevailed, it is that the micro–macro bifurcation is rectifiable since a well-specified general equilibrium model describes the behavior of all economic agents in an economy and *a fortiori* describes the behavior of those agents when they are considered generically, as representative sectoral agents (consumers, capital goods producers, etc.).

Despite this consensus most economists, when distinguishing between microeconomics and macroeconomics, will talk about the level of aggregation at which the various models work. As H. A. John Green [1977] has written: "It is clear that macroeconomics, by its very nature, involves aggregation" [in Harcourt, 1977, p. 179]. In microeconomics the emphasis is on individual behavior, actions of households and firms, and choice calculus. In macro-economics, those same units are treated as aggregates: all households generate a demand for consumer goods, for instance. Consequently the translation from micro to macro necessitates aggregation rules which enable the choice-theoretic household demands for consumer goods to be combined into an aggregate consumption function. Just as at the individual level prices, tastes, and income are needed to generate demand curves, so too at the macro level some "appropriate" real concept explains real consumption demand. Consistency requires that individuals are sufficiently similar so that their behaviors may be summed.

Yet reflection will suggest that microeconomics is not in fact the study of *completely* disaggregated individual behaviors, since the concept of a market price necessitates the existence of a market, which already embodies aggregate interactions. One cannot simply use the concept of aggregation to distinguish microeconomics from macroeconomics. Instead we should examine and categorize the different kinds of inquiries that concern micro and macro theorists.

When phrased in this fashion the level of output becomes a crucial variable. For Keynes the distinction was between value theory which worked with a given level of output, and monetary theory which worked to determine the total level of output.

> The division of Economics between the Theory of Value and Distribution on the one hand and the Theory of Money on the other hand is, I think, a false division. The right dichotomy is, I suggest, between the Theory of Individual Industry or Firm and of the rewards and the distribution between different uses of a *given* quantity of resources on the one hand, and the Theory of Output and Employment as a whole on the other hand [Keynes, 1936, p. 293].

In somewhat more modern terms, microeconomics is the study of (generalized) resource allocation and macroeconomics is the study of the level of economic activity.

In common usage, the questions are somewhat different in texture and intention in microeconomics and macroeconomics. Whether one uses micro models or macro models is a matter of what question is being posed: asking "What would be the effect of a ten per cent increase in the tax on cigarettes?" is not in itself sufficient to determine which model should be used. If the effect of that tax on cigar purchases is sought, a micro model would be appropriate. If the effect on U.S. employment is sought, a macro model would be appropriate. In principle, however, both questions could be phrased in a neo-Walrasian system. Many micro questions, for which partial equilibrium models could be constructed, are embedded naturally in a full ADM system. Some macro questions are also "answerable" using an ADM model. From the point of view of the neo-Walrasian synthesis, while everything can be technically well-posed in a neo-Walrasian model, practical answers to practical questions require the analyst to suppress the complexity of interaction to gain the richness of specificity. An increase in the U.S. cigarette tax may indeed affect British textiles, but the question was about its effect on U.S. cigar sales. So, too, an increase in the U.S. monetary base could affect the relative wage differential between barbers and hair stylists in Durham, North Carolina; in principle it could, in fact we seldom care.

For economists who argue this way, and this would include many neo-Walrasians and Keynesians, the neo-Walrasian ADM model is immensely powerful. Calling it a "microfoundations for macroeconomics" does it an injustice since it is not a bridge between two distinct bodies of knowledge. It in fact is coextensive with both micro and macro, each being a particularization by way of different *ceteris paribus* statements.

General systems theory

It may seem curious that general equilibrium theory, even in the extended sense that economists use the term today, should guide the insights that we have about economic processes. Explanations go deeper than assertions about Walras' influence, the demise of Marshallian and English economics, and the growing professional influence of economists who believe in the hypothetico-deductive mode of inquiry based on the construction of mathematical models.

General systems theory (G.S.T.), of which general equilibrium theory is but a specification to certain economic problems, has existed for many years. As one of its originators, Ludwig Von Bertalanffy has described it,

> G.S.T. is intended to elaborate such principles as apply to "systems" in general, irrespective of their particular kind, the nature of their component elements, and the relations

or "forces" between them. It thus provides a superstructure of theory generalized in comparison with the conventional fields of science. It is capable of giving exact definitions to many notions such as, for example, wholeness, interaction, progressive differentiation, mechanization, centralization, dynamic and homeostatic (feedback) regulations, teleological behaviour, etc., which recur in all biological, behavioral, and social fields, have had some vitalistic or mystical flavor, and were not accounted for in the so-called "mechanistic" approach. In such a way, G.S.T. accounts for the isomorphy of theoretical constructs and of the corresponding traits of reality in the diverse fields of science [Von Bertalanffy, 1960, p. 69].

G.S.T., then, looks for, and finds, many structural similarities among fields of scientific analysis. To the extent that G.S.T. is a constructive approach to inquiry, general equilibrium theory in economics becomes rooted not just in the particular traditions that have generated the multi-fold extensions of the Arrow–Debreu–McKenzie model, but in the very structural unities of science itself. To attack general equilibrium theory in economics as a legitimate model of reasoning is to *simultaneously* deny homeostatic reasoning to psychologists and morphogenic analysis to the biologist. To argue that G.S.T. is inapplicable to economics is to negate claims that economics is a science. There may of course be some who would argue that the panoply of activities that constitute scientific endeavor "ought" not to characterize economics, but such individuals probably are uninterested in economic theory and are thus uninvolved in these kinds of discussions.

A more interesting criticism of G.S.T. would grant its unifying power in science, and in economics, but argue that the "power" has been contrived to guarantee success. On such reasoning G.S.T. is powerful *because* it is tautological and thus its insights are wholly semantic.

In spirit this kind of remark recalls E. P. Wigner's lovely essay

"On The Unreasonable Effectiveness of Mathematics in the Physical Sciences" where he uses the analogy of a person facing a thousand locked doors while holding in his hand a collection of a thousand keys. On trying keys in locks he finds, to his pleasure, that the key he tries in any particular door opens that lock. As Wigner remarks, "Our man may be forgiven if he begins to question the unique correspondence between keys and locks" [1969, p. 124].

A general systems theory, like the neo-Walrasian ADM model in economics, is more than a particular structure to model a particular situation. As indicated in Chapter 2, the neo-Walrasian system has some claim to primacy among economic models since various specifications of it, and extensions of its range, have generated progressively fruitful sequences of useful models in a variety of subdisciplines of economics.

From this point of view, neo-Walrasian general equilibrium theory is not a theory in the same sense as, say, the "theory of the second-best," or the "theory of demand." General equilibrium analysis is not *the* theory of the microfoundations of macro-economics. Instead, the ADM structure is a metatheory, or an investigative logic which, since it is used to construct all economic theories, must necessarily be used to examine "microfoundations of macroeconomics" models.

This argument is a fairly strong one, and many economists will be uncomfortable with it to the degree that they deny the usefulness of neo-Walrasian analysis in some contexts. The micro–macro division does seem real, not contrived. We are not however claiming a simple reductionism whereby both micro and macro theory are particular realizations of the ADM model.

Instead, we are suggesting that general equilibrium theory, the kind of general systems theory that economists have developed, is the appropriate logic to investigate the compatibility between microeconomics and macroeconomics. When it is argued that a number of macroeconomic concerns are *logically* incompatible with the ADM framework (uncertainty, disappointed expectations, etc.) and thus cannot be reconciled with microeconomic structures, we must reply that the ADM theory must then be modified, not abandoned. Our aim is not a universal all-encompassing general equilibrium model. As René Thom has noted:

> To each partial system, relatively independent of the environment, we assign a local model that accounts qualitatively and, in the best cases, quantitatively for its behavior. But we cannot hope, a priori, to integrate all these local models into a global system. If it were possible to make such a synthesis, a man could justifiably say that he knew the ultimate nature of reality, for there could exist no better global model. For myself, I think this would be extravagant pretension; the era of grand cosmic synthesis ended, very probably, with general relativity, and it is most doubtful that anybody will restart it, nor would it seem useful to attempt to do so [Thom, 1975, p. 7].

In its most productive form, this argument leads to the suggestion that the micro–macro distinction itself has been badly posed. There certainly is a bifurcation of theoretical models, but it is not recognizable in the language of aggregation, nor in differences in the assumptions made about the quantity of output.

If we consider the usual approach to constructing ADM systems, it is apparent that an organizing feature of them is the question "how is it possible for a decentralized, individualistic system, operated on principles of self-interest, to produce coherent or coordinated outcomes?" All the assumptions which ensure existence of an equilibrium are just *sufficient* conditions to produce an equilibrium. Consequently, we may *not* say that unless we have perfect competition in a real economy, equilibrium cannot exist. Rather, we must argue that competition is likely to induce systemic coherence, to produce coordination successes.

From this perspective *most of the traditional microeconomic concerns are embedded in models that either assume or produce coherent outcomes.* A simple supply and demand model generates results which suggests that price adjustment coordinates individual behavior in a market; it disseminates information and helps to pre-reconcile choice.

Still speaking intuitively, macroeconomics has been involved with questions like unemployment, inflation, and control of economic aggregates, and thus *its domain of discourse is system-incoherence, or the failure of the economic system to produce automatically well-coordinated outcomes.*

If this is granted, economists have tried to cut economic phenomena into micro and macro when, in fact, the appropriate "cut" is between models of coordination success and models of coordination failure. Topics like imperfect information, transactions costs, and expectations adjustment problems, which have a long history in the monetary theory literature, have only recently been examined from a microeconomic perspective, and they frequently appear in generalized neo-Walrasian models which discuss microfoundations of macroeconomics. If the micro–macro distinction is based on the level of aggregation, these studies are unnatural in the sense that there is nothing inherent, in the move from disaggregated systems to aggregated ones, that seems to force the economist to investigate information costs or transactions cost or expectations. If, on the other hand, relatively costless information induces coordinated behavior, and costly information produces market incoherence, then information costs are properly one element of the now misnamed "microfoundations" puzzle.

Those last few chapters in any microeconomic text on "market failures" are thus not an afterthought, but may be seen as the proper elements of the bridge toward macroeconomic theory where coordinated (e.g., full-employment) outcomes appear, if at all, as either accidents or policy goals. It is thus easy to understand why many macroeconomists are uncomfortable with the neo-Walrasian synthesis. Quite simply, the rules of the ADM modelling game ensure that coordination success will occur. The assumptions were designed as sufficient conditions to product coherent outcomes. Why be surprised that the macromodels induced from ADM structures are uninteresting in the sense that unemployment can only be generated as a model conclusion by theoretically *ad hoc* imposition of wage rigidity, disequilibrium behavior, money illusion, liquidity traps, *et hoc genus omne*? If macroeconomics is properly the study of coordination failure, models which necessitate thinking about the economy as normally producing coherent outcomes must appear strange indeed.

Our insights can be guided by the observation that the *"microfoundations of macroeconomics" must be coextensive with classes of models that are designed to produce both coordination successes and failures, models which can generate outcomes that are fully coherent on some occasion and which, on others, are sufficiently chaotic as to require explicit policy control.*

This kind of economic analysis is not neo-Walrasian. It is based on the work of Robert Clower and Axel Leijonhufvud, work which we must now consider in a bit more detail.

Robert Clower

In many ways, the publication of Clower's "The Keynesian Counter-Revolution" paper in 1965 marked the first serious internal challenge to the neo-Walrasian synthesis of micro and macro.

Clower's argument was brutally simple:

(1) All neo-Walrasian models have structurally similar feasible choice sets defined by the appropriate budget constraints.
(2) In neo-Walrasian analysis, since no trades are carried on except at equilibrium prices, the constraint on household purchases is *realized* income.
(3) Since prices only "existed" in equilibrium, Walras' Law always holds.
(4) Consequently, unemployment is impossible unless there are market rigidities or failures.
(5) Thus, "either Walras' Law is incompatible with Keynesian economics, or Keynes had nothing fundamentally new to add to orthodox economic theory" [Clower, 1970, p. 278].[1]

Clower recognized that the neo-Walrasian synthesis had come

---

[1] Page references to the Clower papers are those in [Clower, 1970].

to mean the affirmation of the truth that Keynes made no theoretical contribution. For Clower, on the other hand, Walras' Law was nonsense in the macroeconomic context. Clower introduced what he termed "the dual decision hypothesis": (1) "if current income receipts do not impose an operative constraint on household spending decisions," usual demand functions can be derived and Walras' Law holds; (2) if, however, current income is a binding constraint, then constrained demand functions emerge from the modified budget constraint. The result is "the dual-decision hypothesis effectively implies that Walras' Law, although valid as usual with reference to *notional* market excess demands, is in general irrelevant to any but full employment situations. *Contrary to the findings of traditional* (neo-Walrasian) *Theory, excess demand may fail to appear anywhere in the economy under conditions of less than full employment*" [Clower, 1970, p. 292].

How much of the (possibly flawed) neo-Walrasian synthesis depended on the rather primitive monetary-theoretic structure of the models and how much depended on the portion of the analysis which could be carried out in a barter setting? Put another way, could macroeconomic insights be gained from non-monetary neo-Walrasian models?

Clower's 1967 paper, "A Reconsideration of the Microfoundations of Monetary Theory" attempted to show that the neo-Walrasian system produced a "conception of a monetary economy . . . [which] is empirically and analytically vacuous."

Recall that for Patinkin, and for Lange and Hicks before him the choices embodied in the budget equation state that the value of net trades equals the difference between desired and initial fiat money holdings. But, this "familiar budget constraint effectively admits as feasible trades all pairwise combinations of commodities that are traded in the economy." However, goods never trade against goods directly in a monetary economy; they only trade against money.

Clower argued that these choice problems are best handled by working with two constraints on choice behavior, not one. There is an expenditure constraint which "asserts that all (net) purchase offers must be backed by a readiness to supply money in exchange," so that *"The total value of goods demanded cannot in any circumstances exceed the amount of money held by the transactor at the outset of the period."* The income constraint, on the other hand, "asserts that all (net) sale offers involve a demand for just one other commodity, namely money, in exchange" [Clower, 1970, p. 209].

The basic idea generating the results of both Clower papers is that in Keynes' monetary-production economy, choices involved money trades. These trades were out-of-equilibrium in the sense that the prices which transactors faced might never convey the information that unemployed resources could be more fully employed. In a phrase, Keynesian problems were disequilibrium problems not well-handled in a neo-Walrasian framework.

This message was already explicit in Patinkin's discussion of points off the supply and demand curves for labor. There was little in Patinkin, however, which suggested in a rigorous fashion how the Keynesian involuntary unemployment problems could be directly traced to the modelling difficulties hidden in the neo-Walrasian system. Clower's distinction between notional and effective demands shifted the attention of the theorists to expectations problems, disequilibrium behavior, and the information content of prices as an efficient allocative mechanism. Clower's insistence on a unique role for money reinvigorated study of the differences between barter and monetary economies and helped combat the view that money didn't matter in macroeconomics because numeraires don't matter in neo-Walrasian systems.

In a more detailed fashion, these insights were developed by Axel Leijonhufvud, to whose work we now turn.

Leijonhufvud's development

The many and interrelated contributions of the author of *On Keynesian Economics and the Economics of Keynes* cannot be suggested in these few pages; our focus is on the microfoundations structure of Leijonhufvud's analysis. In his first (*AER*) major writing on this theme, he noted [Leijonhufvud, 1967] that to generate a Keynesian system from a neo-Walrasian model, "it is sufficient only to give up the . . . strong assumption of instantaneous price adjustments . . . To make the transition from Walras' world to Keynes' world, it is thus sufficient to dispense with the assumed *tâtonnement* mechanism . . . To be a Keynesian, one need only realize the difficulties of finding the market-clearing vector" [in Clower, 1970, pp. 300–2].

In this early statement, the root of the unemployment problem to Keynes was "inappropriately low prices of augmentable non-money assets relative to both wages and consumer good prices. Relative values are wrong" [in Clower, 1970, p. 303]. For those assets, there is no auctioneer adjusting their prices. On the supply side, producers expectations are inelastic, and on the demand side, organized financial markets fail to provide the information that investors would need to forecast future profitability of those capital goods. In this disequilibrium world, information failures are rampant.

In his much praised 1968 book, Leijonhufvud elaborated on these themes. He used Alchian's analysis of the role of uncertainty about demand in the generation of unemployed resources, and Clower's idea of an income-constrained process which exacerbated the effects of that unemployment, to show that " 'reconciling competition with unemployment' appears as a 'riddle' only when 'competition' is implicitly equated with 'perfect information' " [p. 102]. In brief, it is not any rigidity or inelasticity that explains Keynes' view of unemployment. The neo-Walrasian system, with its focus on the possibility of prereconciled choice through a static analysis of existence of equilibrium, deluded itself when it moved to dynamic analysis of disequilibrium states. The laws of motion of the system were given by tatonnements whose only concrete realization was in terms of a fictitious auctioneer. Without an auctioneer, were there in fact mechanisms which "cleared" the various markets? Even if an equilibrium (with all resources fully employed) did exist, there might not exist mechanisms in a decentralized market economy to provide the information (*a*) to preclude disequilibrium trading and (*b*) to enable transactors to carry out their plans in a consistent fashion.

Leijonhufvud argued that for Keynes, the market adjustments were not by price but rather by quantity; real income was a quantity measure which adjusted to equilibrate aggregate supply and demand. The repudiation of price adjustments and the price-adjusting auctioneer was seen by Leijonhufvud as a natural result of Keynes' Marshallian (and thus anti-Walrasian) upbringing:

> In the Keynesian macrosystem the Marshallian ranking of price- and quantity-adjustment speeds is reversed: In the shortest period flow quantities are freely variable, but one or more prices are given, and the admissible range of variation for the rest of prices is thereby limited. The "revolutionary" element in the *General Theory* can perhaps not be stated in simpler terms [p. 52].

The positive, as opposed to the critical, contribution of *On Keynesian Economics and the Economics of Keynes* is best seen in the final chapter, "Two Postscripts." The section on "Communication and Control in Dynamic Systems" provides a coherent vision of the microfoundations problem in its revised form. Leijonhufvud grants that the neo-Walrasian model is a

> kind of Newtonian conception of what the economic system is like [and it] works very well in equilibrium economics . . . [In macroeconomics] however, it tends to bias one's perception of the nature of the problem in a particular direction. When the huge machine does not work as it is supposed to (one tends to infer) it *must be* either because someone has thrown a spanner in the works—"monopolists and unions fix prices"—or because the cogs are slipping someplace—"savers and investors do not respond to interest incentives" [p. 395].

"The varieties of price theory"
In his lengthy January 1974 discussion paper, subtitled "What Microfoundations for Macroeconomics?", Leijonhufvud noted that there were at least two distinct kinds of microeconom-

ics, neo-Walrasian and (neo-)Marshallian, taught and used by the economics profession. He suggested that the macroeconomic structures that each induce will be rather different:

> Walras' general equilibrium model was built up from clearly defined conceptual experiments to market experiments that were as artificial as they were expedient. Marshall, in effect, worked "backwards" from conceptual experiments intended realistically to simulate actual markets—his first and main concern—to comparatively more rough-and-ready individual experiments tailored to serve market theory [p. 5].

The problem results from the set of issues that defines macro-economics as the study of systemic coordination failure. For Leijonhufvud, this failure is described by disequilibrium analysis. Participants in the economic process make decisions based on imperfect information at price–quantity configurations that are *not* equilibrium vectors. Knowledge that one vector could pre-reconcile choices does not answer the question "what process forces arbitrary vectors to converge to equilibrium?"

In his earlier book, Leijonhufvud had answered this by stating that Keynes inverted the Walrasian and Marshallian adjustment speeds of price and quantity. He argued that Keynes used "fast" quantity adjustment and "slow" prices. If we examined a market mechanism, however, we may define a Walrasian process by:

$$\dot{p} = E(p) \tag{w}$$

where $E(p)$ is the excess demand quantity. A Marshallian process would be of the form

$$\dot{q} = E^{-1}(q) \tag{m}$$

where $E^{-1}(q)$ is excess demand price.

This standard pair of adjustment processes have different stability properties, and it was for this reason that Leijonhufvud had been led in his book to suggest that Keynes simply replaced (w) with (m). Unfortunately the two processes are analytically very similar and one cannot make much of their differences in the usual case of downward sloping demand curves and upward sloping schedules. Yet a deeper point is at issue.

The adjustment process (w) is based on an auctioneer type of reasoning which is fundamentally choice theoretic. Individuals adjust quantity decisions based on price signals generated in an extremely queer market. The Marshallian (m) process on the other hand describes a market process of quantity adjustment (rationing) which makes good sense of how, say, a labor market might adjust but leaves unexamined how individual agents could utilize the quantity signals to generate behavior changes. For these reasons Leijonhufvud abandoned his earlier "inversion of adjustment speed" analysis and considered anew the implicit individual and market experiments associated with both (w) and (m).

The formal mathematical symmetry between (w) and (m) obscures the economic experiments which distinguish the Walrasian and Marshallian processes. Assuming the (w) process, and forcing disequilibrium activity, we see that traders have a given price on which to base their quantity decisions, so that

> (m)odelling . . . this family of short-side dominated fix-price cases requires a number of additional analytic decisions. When the supply side is the short one, assumptions have to be formulated about how buyers are rationed and about what relation amounts consumed might bear to amounts purchased, etc. When the demand side is short, analysis requires assumptions about the "rationing" of realized sales and about the relation of amounts produced to those sold [p. 27].

For the (m) process, disequilibrium activity requires quantity observations and price changes, but competitive firms are usually supposed *not* to change prices. Price movement is a market outcome, not an individual adjustment. Implicit in the Marshallian approach, then, is that "it is in the first place a theory about behavior in markets. The theory . . . is phrased in terms of potentially observable magnitudes and attempts roughly to simulate behavior in real-world markets . . . In the standard Marshallian short-run supply and demand diagram, *both* schedules must be interpreted . . . as market equilibrium curves [pp. 34–5].

Since the (*m*) story requires realized rather than planned magnitudes, and since it focuses on the process of adjustment using feedback from market outcomes to individual decisions, the outcome of the (*m*) process will describe *ex post* coordination successes in contradistinction to the (*w*) process which is an *ex ante* view of potentially pre-reconciled choices.

This analysis clarifies the difficulties that neo-Walrasian theory has had, for example, with Keynes' aggregate supply curve which begins with "expected price" or "expected sales proceeds" and is drawn up to relate expected proceeds with the levels of employment which generate those proceeds. In the *ex ante* choice-theoretic language of the neo-Walrasians this is completely opaque. But in Marshallian (*ex post*) terms, we have a complete overlap between expected and realized proceeds since the firms have "internalized" the market behavior that makes their individual behavior consistent with overall adjustment. Hence "one is at liberty to substitute realized (*ex post*) for expected (*ex ante*) magnitudes and hence to speak of expectations as if they referred to 'points' rather than 'schedules' " [p. 44].

The problem is not "resolvable" in any simple fashion. If microeconomics deals with systemic coordination and macroeconomics with systemic failure, we must not get trapped into either/or choices for adjustment processes. "Notional magnitudes are derived from a Walrasian *ex ante* construction; the determination of effective magnitudes requires reliance on Marshallian *ex post* realizations. In analytic construction the theory of effective demand [macro] is basically Marshallian, but the diagnosis of effective demand *failures* depends on the juxtaposition of 'notional' Walrasian and 'effective' Marshallian states" [p. 46].

We are left, then, with some severe difficulties. If neo-Walrasian analysis is to provide a microfoundations for macroeconomics, it must examine actual disequilibrium behavior at both individual and market levels in radically different ways. If neo-Marshallian analysis is to model macroeconomic processes, there must be some individual behaviors that not only are consistent with the market stories, but moreoever are mutually consistent in a general equilibrium sense. As we shall see in Chapter 7, only the neo-Walrasian "extensions" have appeared in the recent literature.

Before leaving this point it should be noted that the Marshallian story of market adjustment may be "easier" to tell in a world where *firms* have considerable market power, since in that case there is less of a discrepancy between individual and market experiments on the supply side. Eichner's [1974] attempt to construct the micro–macro interrelationship for oligopolies can thus be read as a Keynesian attempt to bypass the difficulties that the neo-Walrasian view of competition induces. There is, however, no real "notional" process at work to mark off the potential benefit of systemic coordination.

A new set of questions

In his more recent work, Leijonhufvud has returned to those questions of coordination failures that appeared as a *leitmotif* in his book. In both "Effective Demand Failures" and "Schools, 'Revolutions,' and Research Programmes in Economic Theory," he has focused more on the macroeconomic content than on the potential reconciliation of individual and market experiments. The overall problem is encapsulated in a passage he quotes from Haavelmo to introduce the former paper:

> There is no reason why the *form* of a realistic model (the form of its equations) should be the same under all values of its variables. We must face the fact that the form of the model may have to be regarded as a function of the values of the variables involved. This will usually be the case if the values of some of the variables affect the basic conditions of choice under which the behavior equations in the model are derived [Haavelmo, 1960, p. 205].

The question of "what microfoundations for macro" thus takes a new direction. It is no longer a case of neo-Walrasian generalizations of the induced macromodel à la Patinkin. Neither does it entail building a non-Walrasian choice theory to slip under the edifice of Keynes' analysis. Rather the research strategy suggested by these observations entails the creation of a model, or family of models, that produce neo-Walrasian outcomes, coordinated outcomes, within a "corridor" of small perturbations. Outside that "corridor" effective demand failures are rampant. "In simpler terms, consider a system that within certain bounds around the equilibrium path will 'home in' in the way presumed in pre-Keynesian economics. Outside this 'corridor' its behaviour is sluggish and, well outside, the forces emphasized in Keynesian theory predominate entirely" [Leijonhufvud, 1976, p. 102].

The problem is that such a heuristic for model-selection really does not exist; there has been no work done along such lines. With some pessimism Leijonhufvud noted:

> Mathematical general equilibrium theorists have at their command an impressive array of proven techniques for modelling systems that "always work well." Keynesian economists have experience with modelling systems that "never work." But, as yet, no one has the recipe for modelling systems that function pretty well most of the time but sometimes work very badly to coordinate economic activities. And the analytical devices and routines of neo-Walrasian general equilibrium theory and Keynesian theory will not "mix" [Leijonhufvud, 1976, p. 103].

Part II

Introduction

In this part attention will be directed to the various ways in which general equilibrium theory has been, and is being, modified to provide a conceptual base for the formulation of macroeconomic concerns.

Two major approaches can be identified: the first focuses on interdependent optimization by the various agents, the second is more concerned with the mechanisms for exchange or transactions. Abusing both language and history a bit, the former will be termed (neo-)Walrasian analysis, the latter (neo-)Edgeworthian. A further bifurcation will be between equilibrium theory and disequilibrium theory, or whether the analysis is directed to the possibility of pre-reconciled choice or the attainment of terminal states in real time.

There are thus four "pigeonholes" in which to place recent and current work. The taxonomy consists of Walrasian equilibrium (Chapter 6), Walrasian disequilibrium (Chapter 7), Edgeworthian equilibrium (Chapter 8), and Edgeworthian disequilibrium (Chapter 9).

6

Walrasian equilibrium models

It may be useful to recall the outlines of the Arrow–Debreu–McKenzie general equilibrium model, since this can be regarded as the starting point for subsequent work.

(1) There is a class of agents, called consumers, who have preferences over different bundles of final goods.
(2) The consumer preferences are sufficiently regular so that preferences can be represented by utility indicators.
(3) Consumers' income comes from sale of factor services and distributed profits of firms.
(4) Members of another class of agents, called firms, have preferences over output configurations, which lead to profits.
(5) Consumers, taking product and factor prices as given, attempt to maximize utility subject to their income constraint.
(6) Firms, taking product and factor prices as given, attempt to maximize profits subject to a technology constraint.

Under a variety of economic restrictions it can be shown that there exists a set of factor prices and product prices such that, if consumers and firms were to simultaneously optimize at those prices, the output and purchase of goods that would result entails those same prices. That is, there exists a set of prices (a competitive equilibrium) that could logically reconcile the potentially conflicting choices of all the economic agents. (The allocation of goods that corresponds to the competitive equilibrium is called the competitive allocation.)

This basic construction is far from concerns about speculative demands for money, real versus nominal interest rates, and flexible versus naive accelerators. Consequently, it becomes important to add on assumptions potentially more germane to macroeconomic issues to see what sorts of conclusions emerge. For example, Patinkin's work cited earlier had as a theme the appropriate sort of manner by which money could be introduced to this system in an essential fashion. His solution was based on the idea that agents derived current services from wealth, and thus real money balances constrained the choices that economic agents made. The resulting competitive equilibrium could then be examined for its comparative static implications, and those implications (like monetary neutrality) were essentially macroeconomic.

But as pointed out in Part I, macroeconomic theory requires a much more detailed equilibrium concept to discuss expectations, portfolio choice, and financing investment, for example. Consequently there has developed a literature, based quite securely on the ADM model, which attempts to develop some of those concerns.

The major lessons of macroeconomics suggest first that the ADM model be extended to the future; questions about uncertainty and intertemporal linkages begin to appear in a natural context. One set of such extensions was done in the 1960s, and since it is this extended ADM model that is generally considered standard, it is as well to review it here.

> The basic idea is that commodities are to be distinguished, not only by their physical characteristics and by the locations and dates of their availability and/or use, but also by the environmental event in which they are made available and used . . . The description of the "physical world" is decomposed into three sets of variables: (1) decision variables, which are controlled (chosen) by economic agents; (2) environmental variables, which are

> not controlled by any economic agent; and (3) all other
> variables . . . A state of the environment is a complete
> specification (history) of the environmental variables . . .
> An event is a set of states [Radner, 1970, pp. 454–5].

Since contracts can be written for delivery of a good subject to an event's occurrence, one can create, by combination, contracts for "contingent" commodities. Consumers and procedures are assumed to behave in a standard fashion and

> An equilibrium of the economy is a set of prices, a set of
> production plans (one for each producer), and a set of
> consumption plans (one for each consumer) such that (a)
> each producer's plan has maximum present value in his
> production possibility set; (b) each consumer's plan
> maximizes his preferences within his consumption
> possibility set, subject to the additional (budget)
> constraint that the present cost of his consumption plan
> not exceed his present net worth; (c) for each commodity
> at each date in each elementary event, the total demand
> equals the total supply [Radner, 1970, p. 455].

The price system that emerges can be interpreted, as Radner shows, as a two-part system involving payments for events, and payment for commodities subject to those events, much like the sum of insurance premiums and spot prices for the event in question. Recognize that this system does *not* wait until events have occurred for transactions to take place. It rather investigates whether one can *now* co-ordinate all the agents' plans subject to state-of-the-world uncertainty.

The main difficulty with this construction is easy to comprehend: "[This ADM model] clearly requires that the economic agents possess capabilities of imagination and calculation that exceed reality by many orders of magnitude . . . [and] the theory requires in principle a complete system of insurance and futures markets which appears to be too complex, detailed, and refined to have practical significance" [Radner, 1968, p. 45].

Such issues had only begun to be faced prior to the mid 1960s, but this fact was not a result of special obtuseness on the part of theorists, but rather because the issues were difficult to formulate and embed in the standard neo-Walrasian corpus. Through this period general equilibrium theorists had been following the internal logic of the subdiscipline: models were created, criticized, and reformulated. These exercises were not of the sort that could be easily popularized; they were not on the order of "the models assume perfect competition, the world isn't that way, thus the models are useless." Instead the models were put through more detailed and rigorous tests.

Expectations and uncertainty in multimarket models were examined early. Papers by Arrow and Alain C. Enthoven [1956] and Arrow and Marc Nerlove [1958] indicated that the inclusion of expected future prices, and reasonable mechanisms by which expectations could be modified, hardly perturbed the standard results. The individual primarily identified with such "uncertainty" questions, Roy Radner, was able to determine the precise point at which the Arrow–Debreu model would fail to provide a mechanism to allocate resources efficiently under uncertainty. He showed that "if economic decision makers are uncertain about the environment, and if their information is about the environment, then even if they have different information, a once-and-for-all futures market in conditional contracts can achieve an optimum allocation of resources, relative to the given structure of information" [Radner, 1968, p. 57].

However, if agents are uncertain about other agents' behavior, *so that strategic reasoning intrudes*, no equilibrium may exist even *with* complete futures markets.

This problem is severe. As argued in Chapters 3 and 5, there are ways to present Keynes' work which force the interpretation that macroeconomics deals with coordination failures induced by the dark forces of uncertainty and time, and that money serves to keep these monsters at bay only imperfectly. As Arrow and Hahn state, at the end of *General Competitive Analysis:*

> The Keynesian revolution cannot be understood if proper account is not taken of the powerful influence exerted by the future and past on the present and by the large

modifications that must be introduced into both value theory and stability analysis, if the requisite futures are missing . . . [Keynes] was certainly right in arguing that the theoretical evidence to be adduced from constructions in which these problems did not arise is not relevant [p. 369].

We must be extremely careful not to claim more for the extended (state-of-the-world uncertainty type) ADM model than is actually present. Equilibrium, in the neo-Walrasian program, had a very well-defined meaning as a set of prices and agent plans that could *logically* pre-reconcile the conflicting desires of the market participants. An equilibrium, were it somehow to become established, would not involve any incentives for agents to change any of their current behaviors. Those behaviors, though, are manifest in markets, and we must have "enough" markets to mediate all the relevant plans. The real-time world, without a full array of futures markets, has only a few goods, called assets, which have the property that they yield services over time. Examining models of such a world presents a horde of difficulties, not the least of which is "what do we mean by equilibrium?"

Time and money

For Keynes, uncertainty about the future and the necessity for dealing explicitly with the resulting expectations problems was a major difference between "classical" theories and his own theory of effective demand. In his 1937 lectures Keynes wrote "If I were writing my book again I should begin by setting forth my theory on the assumption that short period expectations were always fulfilled; and then have a subsequent chapter showing what differences it makes when short-period expectations are disappointed" [Keynes, Vol. 14, p. 181].

In the context of the ADM structures, this amounts to thinking of an incomplete system in the sense that there are not enough futures markets to enable agents to take action now for all future eventualities. There is a past, a history of the system, and an interactive current structure. Agents form short-period expectations of sales proceeds which limit output and employment choices. The resulting level of effective demand determines income and employment when cojoined to another set of decisions about investments to be made and money to be held. These latter decisions, however, are of a different character since the expectations upon which they are based are long-term ones, and thus not very responsive to the underlying economic behaviors.

We should study this economy through real time as decisions are made, observations by entrepreneurs on the effects of their actions are internalized, new decisions are reached, and so on, all the while recognizing that the world of exogenous data through which this economy flows is a changing one. This kind of dynamic vision is a sequence of economies ... $E_{-2}, E_{-1}, E_0, E_1, E_2$ ... where the decisions taken at $t = 1$ help bring about the E_2 economy, yet $t = 2$ brings about a new set of events, surprises even, which partially falsify the "truths" established in E_1.

If the world were not in flux, and human behaviors were not so susceptible to the psychology of mass behavior, the underlying structure of the world would present no intrinsic problems, for as $t \to \infty$ more and more would become known, more of the "true" situation would be revealed by the mere passage of time. For Keynes, this kind of fixity characterized the "classical" theory, a theory of the long-run, a theory of harmonious ever-more-coordinated activity. Surely such a world, *in the long-run* one with no future, only a past, could be modelled as a certain world; all markets could be considered as markets for current goods. The ADM schema would be a lucid guide to understanding this economic process.

To Keynes, such a preoccupation with the long-run had blinded economists to the very real difficulties of the short-run in which activity occurs. Unemployment is a problem in the short period, and the argument suggests that as each short period is different, though each flows into the next, unemployment can persist and linger confounding the optimistic forecasts of "classical" economists that such short-run events are mere epiphenomena which, too, will pass away.

It is no accident that this way of thinking was natural for Keynes.

His earliest work, under the influence of Russell and Whitehead, was the *Treatise on Probability* which attempted to provide a framework for the theory of induction. This problem involves a sequence of events occurring through time, namely observations which tend to confirm (or fail to falsify) a given hypothesis. *In the limit,* we could say that the chain of inductive evidence "proves" the hypothesis. A string of head–tail observations does not prove that the probability that a given coin will come up heads on the next toss is one half, for we can never *get* to the limit. We can never observe the entire chain *at once*. Making do with partial evidence, using a logic of partial confirmation, is in the nature of finite humanity. The entrepreneur is no less a gambler than the coin tosser, and he must take action now without waiting for the long-run to come to pass.

In this framework that Keynes presented, it is obvious that the connections between the kaleidic short periods commands primary attention [Shackle, 1974]. We have suggested that expectations link E_t and E_{t+1} but many other economic variables come into play as well. The capital stock, inherited from the past, is given and for most purposes can be taken as fixed between periods since the gestation period for a new plant is long and extends over many months or years. Other assets, however, are not so fixed. Money in particular is a glue which holds the various short periods together. As Davidson is the scholar most identified with this line of thought, it is well to use his words:

> Forward contracting is the most important human
> institution yet devised for controlling the uncertain future.
> Since production takes time, entrepreneurs are always
> entering into forward contracts to assure the future costs
> of inputs, and in a non-integrated production chain, into
> sales contracts to assure prices and revenues in the future
> . . . Since the money wage contract is the most ubiquitous
> forward contract in modern economies and since the
> duration of money wage contracts normally exceeds the
> gestation period for the production of most goods, it is the
> human institution of forward labor contracting which

provides a basis for the conventionality of belief in the stickiness or stability in the price of something over time [Davidson, 1977, p. 25].

The fact that contracts are written in terms of money means that it is money which links the various short-run presents. But why money? Why not wheat, or oil, or any other durable asset? Keynes attempted to answer this serious question in Chapter 17, "The Essential Properties of Interest and Money" and Davidson has been clear on the import of this crucial step in Keynes' argument. Briefly, money is liquid, has low (intertemporal) carrying costs, and has an extremely low risk premium. Further, it is easy (cheap) to produce, it is a substitute for other assets, and it is managed by an array of institutions which have some economic power.

These arguments force the conclusion that the kind of numeraire "money" so easily introduced into the extended ADM model is intrinsically different from the "money" which is the stuff of Keynes' economics. It is a credit to the perspicacity of various Post-Keynesians like Leijonhufvud, Clower, Davidson, Minsky, Shackle, S. Weintraub, Kregel, et al., that they have recognized this point.

What is less creditable, however, is to argue that the complete-futures-market ADM structure *in no way* links up with Keynes' concerns except as an irrelevant theory of the long-run. It is well to linger over this point, for it is frequently lost in the "Post-Keynesian vs. neo-Walrasian" polemics.[1]

---

[1] Lest these comments seem exaggerated, the reader should examine the "Discussion" sections of the Harcourt [1977] volume. The printed comments of the various participants suggest that the neo-Walrasians and Post-Keynesians have little desire to communicate. At one point in these discussions, Professor Malinvaud captured the flavor of the disagreements by suggesting that economists can follow one of three strategies:

"(1) Never work with macroeconomic Theories . . .
(2) Look for direct [non-micro based] justification of macroeconomic Theories . . .
(3) Stop being a purist and accept some compromise . . ." [Harcourt, 1977, p. 204]

The record of the conference suggests that there was little willingness to compromise strongly held positions on the part of the Post-Keynesians (Davidson, Harcourt, Nell, Nuti, Asimakopulos).

There is a well-defined concept of equilibrium in the ADM system. This construct involves the possibility of consistency of agent plans and actions. For Post-Keynesians, "equilibrium" can only mean some sort of intertemporal coherence among the various short periods. Kregel's [1976], and Mrs Robinson's [1971] insistence that it is the *process* that must be studied, not the equilibrium, is a plea for the use of a generalized equilibrium notion, one which allows certain variables in the E_t economy to reflect, not hide, the fact that when $t + 1$ is reached, E_t will be shown to have involved inconsistency of inter-agent expectations. Now surely, taking an n-market ADM structure, one could generalize "equilibrium" by saying that the system is in m-equilibrium $(m < n)$ if precisely m markets clear. The long debate of the Keynes–classics period over the term "unemployment-equilibrium" can be reduced to something meaningful by this language. This Keynesian short-period equilibrium, however, makes an extremely weak claim. Given the economy-wide interrelationships brought into focus by any neo-Walrasian model, like the ADM model, it is hard to evaluate the Post-Keynesian assertion that "equilibrium" can have no meaning in Keynes' system.

Further, from the logic of our microfoundations of macro-economics approach, it is necessary to be able to specify the ways in which E_t and E_{t+1} coordinate well in addition to knowing that lack of coordination may produce unemployed resources in each period. What is needed is some kind of generalized, or incomplete, ADM model which we can label E_t, another which we can call E_{t+1} and so on. The problem is to model the linkages between this sequence of models in such a way that the macro-economic claims can be assessed.

For the past decade, precisely such investigations have been the substance of the neo-Walrasian program. Post-Keynesian attacks on this program, because it *used to use* a single complete ADM model to analyze macroeconomic questions, are irrelevant. The criticism of these new developments should be based on the developments themselves, and not on the fact they did not exist ten years earlier.

Consequently the next two sections will survey recent work on sequence economies and temporary equilibrium models and attempt to show how a number of theorists are currently approaching the problem of integrating partial systemic coordination with macroeconomic cooordination failure.

Sequence economies

We thus find it reasonable to require of our equilibrium notion that it should reflect the sequential character of actual economies. But I believe that we require more than that: we want it to be sequential in an *essential* way. By this I mean that it should not be possible without change in content to reformulate the notion non-sequentially. This in turn requires that information processes and costs and also expectations and uncertainty be explicitly and essentially included in the equilibrium notion . . . We have also reached the point where the rather grandiose Arrow–Debreu notion [of equilibrium] gives way to the more "feet on the ground" Keynesian one [Hahn, 1973a, p. 16].

In his paper "Market Equilibrium and Uncertainty," Radner frames the various concepts of equilibrium in terms of a system in which there exists a sequence of ADM models which are incomplete at each date in the sense that "at every date and for every commodity there will be some *future* dates for which *it will not be possible to make current contracts for future delivery contingent on those events*" [Radner, 1974, p. 52].

There are several possible kinds of equilibrium which can conceivably result. First, there is a sequence of short-run or single-period equilibria which requires market clearing of all *current* markets at each date. Second, and a stronger concept, would be to require that this sequence of momentary equilibria converge (perhaps stochastically) to some kind of asymptotic steady state. Finally, one could require intertemporal consistency of the economy in the sense that the various intertemporal plans held by the various agents will generate behaviors that will validate, or at least not falsify, the expectations of the future that generated those particular plans.

Most research has been directed to this last type of equilibrium although some work has been done on the concept of stochastic equilibrium. Radner defines "an equilibrium of plans, prices, and price expectations [as] a set of prices on the first market, a set of common price expectations for the future, and a consistent set of individual plans, one for each trader such that, given the current prices and price expectations each individual trader's plan is optimal for him, subject to an appropriate sequence of budget constraints" [Radner, 1968, p. 290].

For Hahn, this kind of notion implicitly requires that each agent have a "theory" of the future in the sense that he has a model of the economy which is continually being confronted with the data of experience. In these terms, "an economy is in equilibrium when it generates messages which do not cause agents to change the theories which they hold or the policies they pursue" [Hahn, 1973a, p. 25].

The easiest way to approach modelling such an economy is to impose "Perfect Foresight" on the various agents. This is implicit in the requirement of equilibrium that traders have common price expectations, and in fact can be taken as an assumption which will ensure such coherence. This assumption does not, however, require traders to have "point" expectations; subjective probability distributions of future prices can be admitted. It is even possible to allow each trader to have *different* information about the environment and the preferences of other agents.

What is required to establish existence of this type of sequential equilibrium? For a given trader, i, define a consumption–trade plan (x_i, z_i) as *feasible* given price system $p = (p_1, \ldots, p_n)$ if (1) x_i is in i's consumption set; (2) z_i is an allowable commitment in the sense that it represents net deliveries of goods to other traders that could be made; (3) traders do not exceed, in their commitments to deliver goods, more than their endowments minus their consumptions; and (4) at every date, m, $p_m z_{im} = 0$, so budgets balance.[2]

The set of plans (x,z) optimal with respect to given preferences and prices is called the behavior correspondence. An *equilibrium* is thus characterized by (1) admissible prices; (2) a plan for each trader in his behavior correspondence; (3) non-negative net trading; and (4) aggregate budget balance in each period. Reasonable assumptions about trader behavior, similar to the usual ADM model (e.g., continuous and convex preferences, closed and convex consumption sets, etc.), are used to establish equilibrium in this model.

Without the Perfect Certainty assumption we become involved in severe modelling problems which are generating much current research. If markets do not clear at each date, we may examine the idea that the resulting sequence economy is a *stationary* stochastic process:

> If the time interval between dates is short relative to the speed of adjustment of prices, then before prices can adjust to a temporary equilibrium, the economy will already be at the next date, and the environment will have changed. We shall then observe a process of repeated incomplete adjustment, together with stochastic changes in the environment, and the economy will always be in disequilibrium in the sense that markets will never (or rarely) clear. However, such a stochastic process could be in equilibrium in the sense of being stationary [Radner, 1974, p. 76].

This kind of equilibrium is extremely close to the kind of vision that we suggested lay at the core of Keynes' work.

Further, the concept of sequence economies leads naturally to the investigation, at a micro-level, of some established macrotheory concerns. Specifically, the institutional arrangements under which transactions occur in a real economy are often considered by monetary theorists. If it can be shown that an efficient equilibrium in sequence economies necessitates a money that mediates in

---

[2] Note that p_m is an n-vector of mth period prices, and z_{im} is an n-vector of net deliveries in period m.

exchange and/or serves as a store of value (in an uncertainty context), one will have gone some distance to linking monetary theory with allocation theory.

In a series of papers Hahn [1971], [1973b], Mordecai Kurz [1974] and David Starrett [1973] examined modifications of the basic sequence economy model to include a transactions technology, which consists of rules about permissible transactions (e.g., costless spot transactions and costly forward transactions). In general, the resulting equilibrium will be inefficient, although certain assets can be introduced that entail efficiency relative to the cost of the institutions that "run" the asset. Such structures go some way to examining, as an economic question, the existence or nonexistence of markets. This was the concern of Jerry R. Green [1973], who identified particular efficiency-promoting institutions, like the collateral-loan market, which seem inefficient in the context of standard Arrow–Debreu models with a sufficient number of futures markets.

The difficulty with the Perfect Foresight sequence models is that agents are not really permitted to make mistakes in their forecasts. A more realistic approach is to allow mistaken expectations, and the resulting coordination failures, to feed back upon successive rounds of expectations formation. In this case the information structure must be well defined, for "if we examine the situation at time t and suppose that a participant wishes to forecast prices in the future for various states of nature, all previous choices by participants and their outcomes may be relevant, not just prices" [McKenzie, in Intrilligator, 1974, p. 94].

Further, if expectations can be "wrong," we must explicitly face the problem of trader bankruptcy in the models, since "if during one period such an economy establishes a temporary equilibrium in which some consumers borrow from others, there may not exist during the next period a temporary equilibrium at which all consumers could repay their currently maturing obligations" [Stigum, in Intrilligator, 1974, p. 99].

In any event, it should be apparent that the sequential character of Keynes' short-run requires some sort of linkage of temporary equilibrium models so that the actions of agents may be studied directly. The induced macro model will thus possess a number of desirable characteristics from the macroeconomist's perspective, not the least important of which will the possibility that unemployed resources may appear in a well-defined equilibrium state.

Most recent work has in fact focused on sequence economies *without* the Perfect Foresight assumption. These models are usually called models of *temporary equilibrium* and their properties are becoming considerably more important in the study of microfoundations problems.

Temporary equilibrium

Although Stigum [1969] reintroduced the Hicksian temporary equilibrium model in the late 1960s, it was Grandmont's paper "On The Short-Run Equilibrium in a Monetary Economy" [1971] that has generated recent activity.

Consider an exchange economy in which money is the only intertemporal asset. Each trading period, indexed by time t, will involve exchange of perishable goods and money. In each new period traders have an endowment of goods, w_t, and stock of money held over from the last period, m_{t-1}. If in the tth period prices p_t are given, each trader must choose a one-period consumption plan q_t, and an amount of money m_t to carry forward. Consequently, each trader must forecast, or expect, certain prices p_{t+1} in the next period in order to make a decision, and these expectations are subjectively certain price distributions which are based on all past prices $p_t, p_{t-1}, \ldots$ Since p_t itself was established by previous forecasts, expectations can be "collapsed" to a function $\psi(p_t)$, which takes values in P_{t+1}, the price simplex of period $t+1$ (i.e., $P_{t+1} = \{p_{i,\,t+1} : \sum_{i=1}^{n} p_{i,\,t+1} = 1\}$.

If utility can be represented by an intertemporal utility indicator $u(q_t, w_{t+1})$, and w_{t+1} is certain, the trader's problem is "to maximize $u(q_t, q_{t+1})$ subject to $p_t q_t + m_t \leq p_t w_t + m_{t-1}$ and $\psi(p_t)q_{t+1} \leq \psi(p_t)w_{t+1} + m_t$ where q_t, q_{t+1}, m_t are unknown. The optimal solution(s) gives us the trader's demand for consumption goods q_t and money balances m_t, in response to p_t." [Grandmont, 1971, pp. 214–15].

A moment's reflection should convince the reader that the crux of the problem of establishing an equilibrium lies in the expectations formation function. (If expectations are static, so $\psi(p_t) = p_t$ mistakes will continue throughout the sequence and no equilibrium may exist.) Grandmont's central theorem states that, under some novel conditions which bound forward trades, "a short-run market equilibrium exists if the trader's price expectations do not depend too much on current price" [p. 225].

With this model, Grandmont was able to investigate a simple monetary theoretic proposition about the homogeneity of expected utility with respect to prices and money balances; in general, zero-degree homogeneity will *not* be present except in the case that the elasticity of price expectations with respect to current prices is unity. Hence, certain monetary neutrality propositions can be examined in this simple framework.

Establishing continuity of the expectations formation mechanism is the technically difficult part of the various proofs. In all cases, traders have past information on prices and are considered to possess rules which transform their experience into forecasts: these rules may be simple rules-of-thumb or they may be sophisticated applications of classical statistical techniques. Which techniques generate estimates sufficiently well-behaved to permit the expectations function to be "continuous enough" to operate in an existence proof is an open problem.

If we allow the various traders to enter into forward contracts for some of the goods, the additional structure of the model introduces some interesting complexities since a commodity can now be traded spot at time t, forward at t, and spot at $t + 1$, permitting arbitrage to exist. In several papers Green [e.g., 1973] examined this phenomenon and concluded that a temporary equilibrium could exist provided *"there must be some agreement between the agents' expectations about future spot prices"* [Grandmont, 1977, p. 544]. If there were not, the set of potential feasible trades might (a) not be bounded by resource availability and (b) some contracts could not therefore be honored thus bringing in the complication of bankruptcy.

Monetary theory itself is certainly open to the temporary equilibrium approach. In a series of papers Grandmont and Laroque [1973, 1975, 1976a, 1976b] introduced an agent (a bank) which "issues fiat money by open market purchases or sales on long term bonds" [Grandmont, 1977, p. 130]. Traders in this model hold either real assets—n durable goods—or pairs of financial assets, money and bonds, where the latter is a bank promise to pay one unit of money each period. Consumption goods are also present in each period. The assumptions made are similar to those in the simpler model: endowments of consumption goods and assets (held over) in each period t are strictly positive, expectation of future prices are continuous functions of past prices, expected utility is well behaved, and trader activity is optimal with respect to the appropriate constraints for a given monetary policy which determines the quantity of money.

It can be shown that if the bank pegs the interest rate at $r > 0$, then any monetary policy can be linked to a particular temporary equilibrium price vector. It can even be shown that for a sequence of interest rates approaching zero, the trader's demand for money in the corresponding temporary equilibrium will go to infinity, a "Keynesian" liquidity trap: "The economic mechanism leading to this phenomenon is easy to understand. Since expectations are inelastic . . . the traders should be net sellers of bonds when the rate of interest is close to zero. Thus as the rate falls to zero, the bank must create increasing amounts of money to bring the bond market into equilibrium" [Grandmont and Laroque, 1976b, p. 133].

The research program in temporary equilibrium theory thus involves simple and incomplete ADM structures indexed by time, assets (both financial and real) which link period to period, and an optimizing framework appropriate to the resulting sequence of constraints. There are a large number of variant models which can be explored in this context. As Grandmont notes: "More work is needed to include less severely limited planning horizons, a wider variety of financial instruments, and financial institutions such as commercial banks. One can hope, then, to study on a precise basis such monetary issues as the term structure of interest rates ... [and] the role of money as a medium of exchange" [Grandmont, 1977, p. 554].

The major difficulty with these models has been a lack of agreement about the manner in which *firms* should be introduced to create production economies (as opposed to exchange systems). In the temporary equilibrium model with production, the time profile of production is of some importance, and, further, the firm must usually choose specific plans both for financing production and paying out dividends over time.

As Grandmont points out in his survey, however, there are two major problems which arise with the introduction of firms into these models. First, if firms supply bonds (which generate interest paid, in money, out of future sales) to finance current production, there must be some "natural" way to bound the supply of bonds. Yet the expectations of bankruptcy, which in fact restrain real firms, are immensely difficult to model since such fundamental discontinuities in behavior "mess up" existence proofs. Further, without bounds on the supply of new equity, equilibrium in the stock market is tenuous, and this introduces difficulties in establishing propositions about the firms' debt–asset structure.

In a positive vein we can see that the Arrow–Debreu–McKenzie model has been extended in a variety of directions to account for the "real" absence (1) of futures markets for commodities (under certainty) and (2) contingent commodities (under uncertainty). The analysis has "fit-together" ADM markets at different dates and examined not only the variety of equilibrium notions that arise naturally (see Michael Allingham [1973]), but also the way these markets are linked through transactions structures, expectations, information requirements and types of financial assets. This context appears to hold some promise of providing "natural" linkages between the standard theories of resource allocation and those aggregative structures that explicitly analyze the role of financial institutions in a production-time–money world.

More pessimistically, it should also be clear that equilibrium notions are beginning to proliferate, and the simple stories of general competitive analysis must be somewhat recast in order to model the concerns of macro-theorists.

One extensive critique of the temporary equilibrium story as a reconstruction of macroeconomic concerns is due to Hahn, who observed that in the simple ADM concept, "the most striking feature of the short period Walrasian equilibrium approach to Keynesian theory is that it leaves a vast part of the *General Theory* unaccounted for" [Hahn in Harcourt, 1977, p. 27].

As a result, the work of Grandmont et al. at least enables various issues to be posed in a more comprehensive manner. For example, Keynes' concern with money wages being *given* at the start of each short period is intimately bound up with the sort of expectations mechanisms that temporary equilibrium theory seems to require. More importantly, however "a picture has emerged in which prices are set 'at the beginning of the period' and the length of the period is the smallest interval before some price is changed . . . This 'fixed price' model does not strike me as very useful but in any case the short period here is not Keynes' short period" [ibid., p. 35].

Further difficulties abound, Unemployment is discussed, in these various models, by comparing the temporary equilibrium with a competitive equilibrium that would exist were (a) all expectations well-coordinated and (b) money no particular problem. Implicit is the argument that coordination failures result from the "monetary" character of the system. But a variety of models exist to establish the result that "if an equilibrium is a state where rational actions are compatible and if amongst possible actions are included changing of price, then there exist non-Walrasian unemployment equilibria . . . [but] I do not think it useful to call each and every departure from Walras, Keynesian" [ibid., pp. 34–5].

A concluding note

For economists interested in microfoundations of macro-economics the sequence models of temporary equilibrium theory are an extension of the standard ADM structure designed to phrase, and suggest answers to, essentially macroeconomic queries. In terms of coordination success versus failure distinctions between micro and macro, the temporary equilibrium models "load" the failures into monetary theory in the sense that barter economies naturally coordinate well. This may well be false, Clower to the contrary notwithstanding, although the argument cannot be developed until the next chapter.

It is certainly too soon to suggest that temporary equilibrium theory is the True Way. On the other hand, such models do permit analysis of a variety of issues that were traditionally non-questions within the neo-Walrasian program. Whether the answers are coherent to macroeconomists is, at present, perhaps a less important matter than the fact that the questions are leading naturally to joint micro–macro forms of analysis. As a result, we may assert that, at a minimum, general equilibrium theorists have demonstrated quite convincingly that Keynesian macroeconomics cannot be derived from any simple Walrasian microsystem. This is of some consequence. It is difficult, today, for serious macrotheorists to argue against income policies on the grounds that they distort the price signals that enable a (Walrasian) multi-market system to function efficiently. That is not to say that incomes policies are "good things," but rather that they cannot be assessed from a Walrasian perspective, since a Walrasian equilibrium model generates uninteresting macrosystems.

The important lessons are probably methodological. As Edward O. Wilson [1975, p. 28] remarked, in another discipline:

> in Sociobiology, it is still considered respectable to use what might be called the advocacy method of developing science. Author X proposes a hypothesis to account for a certain phenomenon, selecting and arranging his evidence in the most persuasive manner possible. Author Y then rebuts X in part or in whole . . . [A]uthor Z appears as an amicus curiae . . . and so forth seriatim through many journals and over years of time. Often the advocacy method muddles through to the answer. But at its worst it

leads to "schools" of thought that encapsulate logic for a full generation.

Matters are not quite so grim in economics, where postulational–deductive model building is well-established. The danger that Wilson notes, however, will be present for macroeconomics to the extent that the general equilibrium microfoundations of the subject are ignored.

7

Walrasian disequilibrium theory

In *Money, Interest, and Prices,* Patinkin noted that "Keynesian economics is the economics of unemployment *dis*equilibrium. It argues that ... the dynamic process ... is unlikely to converge either smoothly or rapidly to the full-employment equilibrium position. Indeed, [a variety of effects] ... may even render this process unstable" [p. 338].

Ever since this analysis, there has been interest in the dynamic processes of neo-Walrasian theory since, on the surface at least, there is intuitive appeal to the argument that neo-Walrasian systems have coherent (full-employment) states at the termination of their dynamic adjustments, whereas Keynesian systems do not. In any event, the usual observation that Keynesian systems "do not coordinate activity very well" has an easy formalization in terms of "unstable dynamic adjustment mechanisms."

As noted in Chapter 2, this view was not inappropriate to the late 1950s and early 1960s, since mathematical economists had finally established sets of sufficient conditions under which market price adjustment mechanisms, of the tatonnement variety, would be globally stable.

Recall that, in general, the tatonnement can be written as

$$\dot{p} = E(p) \tag{1}$$

where p is a column n-vector of prices, the state variables, and

109

$E(p)$ is the column vector of the n excess demand functions. Suppose that $p^* > 0$ is the (assumed) equilibrium vector, and consider the Liapunov function

$$V(p) = \tfrac{1}{2} \sum_{i=1}^{n} (p_i - \dot{p_i}^*)^2 \tag{2}$$

Certainly $V(p)$ is always non-negative, zero only at equilibrium, and is continuously differentiable. From the discussion in Chapter 2 then, the tatonnement (1) is stable provided $\dot{V}(p) < 0$, so let us compute.

We find

$$\dot{V}(p) = \sum_{i=1}^{n} (p_i - p_i^*) \, \dot{p_i} \tag{3}$$

so, substituting from (1),

$$\dot{V}(p) = \sum_{i=1}^{n} (p_i - p_i^*) E_i(p) \tag{4}$$

or

$$\dot{V}(p) = \sum_{i=1}^{n} p_i E_i(p) - \sum_{i=1}^{n} p_i^* E_i(p) \tag{5}$$

If Walras' Law holds, $\Sigma p_i E_i(p) = 0$ so we are left with the statement that

$$\text{``}\Sigma p_i^* E_i(p) > 0 \text{ implies (1) is stable''} \tag{6}$$

Recognizing that $E_i(p)$ is the difference, in a competitive economy, between demand quantities and supply quantities, (6) is thus equivalent to the statement

> "[(1) is stable when] the *aggregate* excess demand functions satisfy the weak Axiom of Revealed Preference[1] (at least in comparisons between equilibrium and other points)" [Fisher, 1976, pp. 9–10] (7)

Since most stability arguments for the tatonnement reduce to our statement (7), it should be clear that stability is unlikely to arise "naturally," since the Weak Axiom, while it makes good sense for individual behavior, is a remarkably unreasonable restriction to place on aggregate behavior.

[1] For a good statement of this axiom, see [Takayama, p. 283, n. 4].

This little digression is more important than it might appear for a most curious reason. When the first stability theorems appeared it was as if many macro-oriented neo-Walrasians breathed a sigh of relief murmuring "Arrow et al. proved the system is stable, so we don't have to worry any longer." Two passages may suggest the pervasiveness of this kind of thinking:

[The work of Samuelson, Arrow et al.] . . . is the long-delayed, critical, and rigorous analysis of the necessary conditions under which Walras' tatonnement will bring the economy to its equilibrium solution [Patinkin, 1965, p. 540].

No set of reasonably realistic, sufficient conditions for stability of the general equilibrium system has ever been presented; nonetheless, some economists are content to assume that the system is stable on the basis of casual observations of the behavior of modern economies, asserting that since they appear stable, we can safely assume that the general equilibrium system is stable. Such observations do not prove anything, of course, and there is reason to warn against this kind of reasoning . . . Moreover, such arguments may not be altogether free from wishful thinking [Hansen, 1970, p. 35].

Patinkin is surely wrong, confusing sufficient conditions with necessary ones. Hansen on the other hand is keenly aware of the difficulty, yet the next two hundred pages of his rightly-acclaimed text relies on a comparative static type of analysis which is valid *only* if the underlying dynamic process is stable.

The paradox is apparent. Just at the time that mathematical economists were doing away with the tatonnement as a useful adjustment device, the neo-Walrasian synthesis was beginning to take the stability of the process as "given."

Fisher's lovely survey addresses this same point: "As I go on to consider what we know about [stability] and as you are tempted to grow impatient with the sorry state of that knowledge, please bear in mind that every economist [sic] continually behaves as though the unsolved questions I am addressing had long ago been satisfactorily resolved" [Fisher, 1976, p. 5].

The argument that disequilibrium analysis must be at the root of any microfoundations of macroeconomics study is incorrectly formed if it is perceived that the "good" (stable) microeconomics of neo-Walrasian theory can be contrasted to the "bad" (unstable) macrosystems of the Keynesian variety. In fact, stability of equilibrium is problematical in any general equilibrium structure, whether disaggregated as the neo-Walrasian or aggregated as the Keynesian.

The microfoundations analyst has a doubly difficult task, since the study of economic processes out of equilibrium must be compatible with *both* micro and macro insights. It is for this reason that most dynamic analysis must begin with a critique of the tatonnement since, to replace it, the goal must be some process that incorporates its strengths without replicating its weaknesses.

Tatonnement versus non-tatonnement

Economists have always regarded the "law of markets" as a basic fact; that price rises for a good in excess demand and falls for a good in excess supply is taken as a true statement by economists of all persuasions. This partial equilibrium result depends on "nice" demand and supply curves, and thus on perfect competition. Further, there must be some sort of organized market. But how does the price change? Who changes it?

The tatonnement story relies on a central market organizer, an auctioneer, who calls out prices, examines the resulting demand and supply quantity orders that the price elicits from the traders, and changes price to ration or allocate the scarcity. It must be assumed that no trades are actually made until the equilibrium is reached, otherwise the disequilibrium trades change trader income, and hence change demands, which are assumed to be *given* schedules throughout the process.

The tatonnement implicitly assumes what Fisher terms the Present Action Postulate (PAP) which, based on the "assumption that individuals take action to make their excess demand effective . . . involves the assumption that they *can* take such action, which . . . implies that they have something of value which they can and do sell so as to have something to offer when they buy" [Fisher, 1976, p. 7].

This assumption appears unobjectionable if we limit discourse to models of current periods only, but when we extend the analysis to examine future goods, or markets for future goods, we are assuming that individuals can and do take action now to coordinate all plans which extend into the future. The PAP is related to the "no trade except in equilibrium" assumption.

The auctioneer himself raises a host of problems. His primary function is to provide information to the traders, information which consists of a price movement. A demander of ten units can thus know, when price is increased, that his ten unit consumption plan is incompatible with the demands and supplies of all the other agents. The auctioneer as an information disseminator is part of the standard story about "price conveying information," but the auctioneer has at least two other roles.

First, the auctioneer must physically clear the market at the equilibrium price. The traders, when equilibrium is set, only know that the totality of buy orders equals the totality of sell orders. There remains the question of what happens next, or how does the market actually clear? One story requires sellers to deliver goods to the auctioneer who hands them out to the buyers. There are several pure transactions cost problems involved in this tale. If it is costly for the auctioneer to handle goods, and cost is less than proportional to the basket of goods, the auctioneer might like to effect a few large orders rather than many small ones. It might even be worthwhile to reduce the unit price if such an action could induce a few large block trades [Baligh, et al. 1976].

These matters are readily seen to involve little of economic substance. As Shubik notes,

> Real transactions costs [are a red herring] which divert
> attention from the more critical transactions costs which
> are due to information gathering, coding, and decoding
> . . . [They] may well [involve] elegant exercises in
> combinatorics and may even suggest certain optimal

design features for markets . . . [but] the returns from this type of work may not be commensurate with the effort required [Shubik, 1975, pp. 569–70].

The second role of the auctioneer is rather more crucial: a price changes *because* the auctioneer changes it. This leads immediately to the question "why should he?" This is not an aberrant query, for every other agent in the system is basing action on optimizing behavior. What is it that the auctioneer optimizes? "How many angels can dance on the head of a pin?" Apart from the fact that, except in a few stock-type markets where the auctioneer may be approximated by a "specialist," Walrasian auctioneers do not exist. If we apply Occam's Razor to eliminate this proliferation of in-principle-unobservables, we ask "What can replace the auctioneer?"

In response to questions of this sort, theorists began to examine the behavior of disaggregated economic units and to specify with some rigor the precise manner in which these agents might adjust to the disequilibrium signals. Although the term "non-tatonnement" is not descriptive, economists began investigating alternative mechanisms that did not, for example, preclude trade-out-of-equilibrium. The literature that developed with papers by Negishi [1962] and Hahn and Negishi [1962] identified what has come to be called the Hahn-process: an exchange model that permits trading at all prices subject to the proviso "that two individuals exchange if and only if neither suffers a utility loss by so doing and one gains" [Hahn, 1970, p. 2].

The tatonnement process precludes trade-out-of-equilibrium because income effects (distribution shifts) are present if one permits such trading. These effects must be removed to ensure stability. For the Hahn process, however, it is production that causes the trouble, since firms that profit maximize at disequilibrium price ratios will not always be increasing their utility through exchange over the price trajectory. "If we were further to allow for the embodiment of production decisions in some durable concrete objects, the path of the system will at any time be strewn with the remnants of past mistakes" [Hahn, 1970, p. 3].

Assuming the Clower distinction that in a monetary economy only money can purchase goods, speculation may prevent steady increase of achieved utility via the trading process, "For if a household is constrained to use a medium of exchange, it may be willing to exchange one good for money on the supposition that the money so acquired will be used in exchange for some other good. But should the second leg of the transaction fail to materialize . . . [a] speculative element is introduced" [Hahn, 1970, p. 3].

Such analysis suggests that neither simple tatonnement processes nor any utility-increasing process alone can support theories of aggregative behavior in which production takes time and money serves to link the past and present with the future. Indeed, Arrow and Hahn [1971, p. 347] observed that perhaps "Keynes was more concerned with demonstrating a 'failure' of the price [adjustment] mechanism than [with] arguing that there exist no prices that make equilibrium possible. Considering the amount of attention he gave to matters such as expectations and speculation, this is a very plausible interpretation."

It is important to recognize the emergent problem: does the non-tatonnement analysis suggest that economists will eventually find it possible to tell a satisfactory adjustment story, or does it merely illustrate the futility of continuing to work with tatonnement models in a microfoundations context? Notice that even the non-tatonnement approach precludes a variety of detail that is necessary to discuss monetized production economies and the possible ways decentralized markets can fail to coordinate economic activity. Consequently, one problem that has been brought into sharp focus in recent years has been the "auctioneer" construct itself, for it serves to coordinate behavior for both the tatonnement and Hahn processes. Without the auctioneer, "we are faced with the necessity of specifying precisely the forces which shape the producers' demand for goods, and in particular how this demand reacts to these signs" [Hahn, 1970, p. 11].

What can replace the auctioneer? How do prices change in real markets? These questions are seen to be critical for specifying a general equilibrium model that can contribute to the formulation of macroeconomic issues. We may notice that these questions also arose in a partial equilibrium setting in the foundations-of-the-Phillips-Curve literature (see Phelps [1970]) where it was necessary to specify mechanisms of wage changes in a more realistic fashion than could be provided by a labor market tatonnement-cum-auctioneer. Recent work on price adjustment without the auctioneer thus has two parents: Hahn processes with the Clower view of actual vs. notional constraints and the information-search models of labor market behavior. Since a number of issues related to this latter theme have been admirably surveyed by Michael Rothschild [1973], it will suffice to sketch some recent developments in the multimarket framework.

Before we do so, however, we must get a bit more specific about the actual dynamics of non-tatonnement adjustment mechanisms. In particular, consider a price adjustment process like the pure tatonnement (equation (1) above).

We rewrite this as

$$\dot{p}_i = E_i(p, \bar{X}) \qquad i = 1, 2, \ldots, n \tag{1'}$$

to suggest that excess demands are functions of endowments in an exchange model.[2] $\bar{X}$ *is a matrix with columns* $\bar{x}_h$ *representing* endowments of the hth household.

The non-tatonnement or trading process part of the mechanism must tell us how endowments change over time as trades are effected at non-equilibrium prices. Arrow and Hahn [p. 326] present two feasible conditions:

$$p\bar{x}_h(t) = 0 \quad \text{all } h, t \geqslant 0 \tag{2'}$$

$$\sum_h \dot{\bar{x}}_h(t) = 0 \quad \text{all } t \geqslant 0 \tag{3'}$$

"The first of these [equations] establishes that no household can change its wealth by exchange . . . [and] the second confirms that we are in a pure-exchange economy without production" [p. 326].

To specify fully the exchange process, the problem is to identify

---

[2] Thus at every instant of time, the rate of change of the ith price depends not only on prices but endowments as well.

some process that changes endowments *and* satisfies (2′) and (3′); i.e., we seek a function, *G,* which is economically meaningful, and such that

$$\dot{\bar{x}} = G\,(\bar{x},\,p) \qquad\qquad (4′)$$

in other words (4′) is cojoined to (1′) subject to (2′) and (3′).

The Hahn process described above satisfies these requirements. Trade takes place, when feasible, when utility can be increased through trade. Interestingly enough this process entails the result that although

> there may be of course either unsatisfied demand or unsatisfied supply . . . markets are sufficiently well organized that there are not both. In other words, there may be people who wish to sell apples at the current prices and cannot or there may be people who wish to buy apples at the current prices and cannot, but there are not simultaneously both unsatisfied sellers and unsatisfied buyers [Fisher, 1976, p. 13].

For the Hahn process,[3] archetypical of the disequilibrium processes we shall examine later in this chapter, it can be shown that stability of (1′)–(4′) is entailed by stability of (1). Hence, whenever

---

3 The process described in some detail is frequently called the "Hahn-process," to distinguish if from two other non-tantonnement mechanisms, the "Barter Process" and the "Edgeworth Process" (see Takayama, 1974, p. 344). For the Barter process, there is simply a trading rule that embeds equation (2), while an "Edgeworth Process" specifies that trader utility should increase out of equilibrium. For this latter specification, we have in fact a gradient adjustment of utilities and, since both Barter and Edgeworth mechanisms build on the excess demand-price adjustment structure of the tatonnement, their stability is guaranteed by the usual tatonnement stability theorems.

For several reasons, however, we shall argue later (see Chapter 9) that the actual disequilibrium process described by Edgeworth is best modelled *without* a market price adjustment equation. Thus we believe that the term Edgeworth Process, as used to describe a non-tatonnement price dynamic, is misleading. Consequently the utility-gradient price adjustment could be christened the "Candide Process" ("every day, in every way, a trader gets better off and better off"), reserving the term "Edgeworth process" for a family of direct exchange mechanisms to be discussed later. This usage is non-standard, so the reader should be wary.

the underlying price adjustment mechanism is stable, the endowment shuffling process introduces no destabilizing influences. Intuitively, the trader finds that

> outside of equilibrium, the things that he wishes to buy and cannot buy are getting more expensive while the things which he wishes to sell and cannot sell are getting cheaper unless they are already free. Accordingly, he finds himself getting worse and worse off in the sense that his *target* utility, the utility which he expects to get if he can complete all his transactions, is going down . . . [The] sum of such target utilities will serve as a Lyapunov Function [Fisher, 1976, p. 13].

In several ways, the Hahn process is rather a nice one, since it relies on traders meeting and allocating the scarcity by their own disequilibrium activity. However the costs of such trader activity are suppressed in the model. The process really is better thought of as being carried out by the auctioneer, although he is no longer constrained to preclude disequilibrium trades. The reason for this is buried in the assumption that "markets are sufficiently well organized so that there are not both [excess demands and supplies of a good]" [p. 13].

There are many issues that this observation raises. Consequently in the next section we shall examine recent attempts to get rid of the auctioneer altogether. Then we shall look at the so-called neo-Keynesian disequilibrium processes which allocate by quantity rules rather than price rules. Finally, we shall attempt an overview of the remaining unresolved issues.

Disequilibrium with no auctioneer: the Fisher process

With no auctioneer, one must take some care with assumptions about how individual agents actually change prices. In an economy made up of both households and firms, we would like each of the agents to behave as a buyer and seller in at least several of the various markets. Suppose that each agent is a "specialist" in at least one market, so that a firm can be identified with a product it sells, say, or a household with the labor services it can provide.

The interesting thing about distinguishing commodities in this way, however, is that, if one does so, the Hahn process assumption becomes so natural as almost to be compelled ... [for] if a given seller (who is the only one on the supply side of the market for the commodity he sells) finds that he cannot sell as much as he would like to sell at the price he sets, then there are not also buyers (with money) who know about him and would like to buy more from him at that price [Fisher, 1976, p. 23].

There are a variety of technically difficult points connected with this process of which one clearly stands out, namely continuity of the price trajectory. We need some kind of "large number of customers" assumption to ensure that price won't jump by large and discrete moves. Further, since different sellers of the same good are modelled as selling different goods, identical toothpaste might have two or more "market" prices. To get around this issue, also one of continuity, we must suppose that the search of the customers is wide enough so that no arbitrage is possible. It is always possible in this model that a seller of good A, who is also a customer for goods B and C, will observe that only a zero price can clear the A market, but this "bankruptcy" result drops him out of the B and C markets; sellers of B and C then observe discontinuities in the excess demands for their wares. We need, then, some sort of No-Bankruptcy assumption for this auctioneerless Hahn process, which we may call the "Fisher process."

The primary difficulty with this story, however, is not in the technical demands upon the mathematics used, but is rather in the economic conceptualization. Fisher brings this point out clearly in several places, noting

not only is it reasonable to make sellers act while setting such prices just as they would if they were certain that they had set equilibrium prices but also it is hard to suppose that sellers fail to notice that their demand curves are not flat and that the number of searching buyers who attempt to purchase from them depends on the prices that they set ... [It] appears evident that sellers facing a

declining demand curve . . . ought to behave as
monopolists [Fisher, 1976, pp. 24–5].

Fisher concludes his survey of these general equilibrium results
by stating that *"We lack a theory of convergence to equilibrium
based on more reasonable individual behavior largely because we
usually do not know what more reasonable individual behavior is"*
[ibid., pp. 25–6].

We have seen that abandoning the auctioneer *and* the tatonnement simultaneously leads to severe conceptual difficulties. They
are not insurmountable, but rather they appear to lead into the
wilderness of "anything goes." Any process which hopes to
support macroeconomic reasoning must be of the non-
tatonnement variety. Auctioneer-less structures are another issue
entirely, and much recent work has examined, in a partial setting,
the intrusion of monopolistic price setting on the disequilibrium
path.

Questions about "buy-now-versus-look-again," revision of
expectations, informational efficiency and decentralization, and
the role of money play a crucial role. An explicit treatment of the
uncertainty theme in such analysis was presented by Peter A.
Diamond [1971] and, later J. D. Hey [1974]. A somewhat more
complete characterization of the decisions facing the firm was
presented by Katsuhito Iwai [1974] in the context of monopolistic
competition, building on Robert J. Barro's analysis of a monopolistic firm's price adjustment [1972]. A short note by Herschel I.
Grossman [1969] identified the blend of Hahn–Clower–Patinkin
that characterizes such an approach to the microfoundations
problem, while Barro and Grossman [1971] have examined these
issues from an explicitly macroeconomic perspective, focusing on
implications of the adjustment processes for such phenomena as
the multiplier, accelerator, and unemployment. This work links up
with Patinkin's aggregative analysis.

Interplay between individual and market forces places a burden
on the mathematics used to model the adjustment dynamics.
There are difficulties, for example, with using continuous market
excess demand functions in either tatonnement or non-

tatonnement mechanisms if those functions result from the partial adjustment behavior of all the individual agents. The mathematics of such models is extremely delicate and may not be able to support the kind of interrelated individual-cum-market theory of adjustment, which emerges from the Walrasian approach. Further, there is a little that is known about such systems (see P. Champseur, J. Drèze, and C. Henry [1974]).

If the price adjustment schemes discussed here present difficulties, as allocation mechanisms for decentralized disequilibrium modelling, it is understandable that other schemes, based on quantity rationing, might lead to interesting insights. To such models we now turn.

The Drèze-Benassy process

In a series of studies based on the temporary equilibrium concept, a number of French economists have been analyzing what they term "neo-Keynesian disequilibrium" models. As we shall see, this label is rather misleading. We shall identify the structures that have developed with Drèze and Benassy since they have been primarily responsible for generating this line of inquiry.

This basic idea, as outlined by Benassy [1975], following Drèze [1975], lies in considering an economy where money must be the sole medium of exchange: "agents express demands and supplies on a particular market [in terms of money]; then the exchange process takes place, in which each agent realizes a transaction (being eventually rationed) and perceives quantity constraints on his exchange. Then as a function of perceived constraints, he will express new demands on the subsequent markets . . . and so on" [Benassy, 1975, p. 504].

For expositional clarity, this sequential and thus non-tatonnement process is collapsed into a simultaneous tatonnement adjustment in the body of the paper. Since excess demands, $\tilde{Z}_h$, expressed by the ith agent in the hth market need not sum to zero in aggregate, while transactions $\bar{Z}_{ih}$ must equal zero, there must be a rationing scheme "to go from effective demands $\tilde{Z}_{ih}$ to actual transactions $\bar{Z}_{ih}$. We shall assume

$$\bar{\bar{Z}}_{ih} = F_{ih} (\bar{Z}_{1h}, \bar{Z}_{2h}, \ldots, \bar{Z}_{nh}) \qquad (a)$$

with

$$\sum_{i=1}^{n} F_{ih} \equiv 0''^{4} \quad [\text{ibid., p. 505}]. \qquad (b)$$

The analysis is carried through by means of restrictions on the rationing scheme. These restrictions were suggested by the more macroeconomic analysis of Clower and Barro and Grossman, namely

(i) One cannot force any agent to exchange more than he wants . . . [and]

(ii) Individuals on the "short" side (i.e., suppliers if there is excess demand, demanders if there is excess supply) can realize their demands . . . [and]

(iii) All F_{ih} functions are continuous in their arguments [ibid., p. 505].

If each individual is specialized in one good (as in the Fisher process) the question of agent h's perceived transaction constraint, $\bar{\bar{Z}}_{ih}$, is a matter of his observing the demands expressed by all other agents, so

$$\bar{\bar{Z}}_{ih} = G_{ih} (\bar{Z}_{1h}, \bar{Z}_{2h}, \ldots, \bar{Z}_{nh}). \qquad (c)$$

The perceived constraints are assumed to have the properties that (α) if an agent is on the long side of the market, his realized transaction is his perceived constraint; (β) if the agent can fulfill his demand, because he is on the short side say, he may subjectively perceive more possibility for trade in the same direction; and (γ) the G_{ih} are continuous.

The problem is to specify the manner by which the perceived constraints are generated, for they drive the system to new states:

We shall call effective demand for good h, $[\bar{Z}_{ih}]$, the exchange the agent wishes to realize on market h to maximize his utility, *taking into account the exchanges he perceives as feasible on the other markets* . . . What an

---

[4] In other words, (a) actual rationing of transactions depends upon the strength of the agents' demands, and (b) rationing clears the markets.

> individual does is compute an optimal exchange plan,
> taking into account the constraints he perceives on the
> *other* markets, and then announces the trade he wishes to
> realize on market h ... this effective demand is made
> against money [ibid., p. 508].

An equilibrium ("neo-Keynesian equilibrium" in Benassy's terminology) is characterized as a set of effective demands $\tilde{Z}_{ih}$, perceived constraints $\bar{Z}_{ih}$, and realized transactions $\hat{Z}_{ih}$ satisfying (a), (b), (c), (α), (β), and (γ) and the optimization problem.

The characterization of this equilibrium is the central point of the analyses. The major result is that the equilibrium is likely to be inefficient in the sense that some exchange which is feasible and a Pareto-improvement for some set of traders cannot be realized by the quantity-constrained process. The inefficiency is not due to the quantity-constraints or the resulting price-inflexibility, but rather it results from the Clower–Leijonhufvud type assumption that all trades must go through the money commodity.

> This informational failure is clearly due to the particular
> nature of effective demands in a monetary economy, and
> specifically to the fact that information on desired real
> counterparts is not transmitted ... In mathematical terms,
> only $\tilde{Z}_{ih}$, the hth component of each optimizing vector, is
> transmitted, not the remainder of the vector ... The
> ultimate cause of inefficiency [is] ... the extreme
> complexity of the indirect barter exchanges which would
> be necessary without money [ibid., pp. 512–13].

Inefficiency results from the fact that although some direct goods–goods trades are Pareto-improving, there may be no corresponding way to realize the goods–money→money–goods sequence necessary to effect the improvement. If the first leg of the transaction fails to materialize, the inefficiency "spills over" to spoil the second leg, reminiscent of Leijonhufvud's "deviation amplifying feedback loops," or "multiplier effects."

How reasonable are these "rationing" rules? In a related paper, Grandmont, Laroque, and Younes [1976] show that the short-side quantity rationing process rules, which lead to (neo-Keynesian)

"K-equilibria", can be derived from the imposition of recontract stability in the sense that any set of agents cannot improve their holdings through trade. Similarly, Böhm and Levine [1976] show that an equilibrium of the neo-Keynesian type, in models of temporary equilibrium with quantity-rationing, "corresponds to a best response strategy equilibrium of each individual agent, exhibiting a Nash property in desired net trades . . . [Such equilibria] clearly describe situations of Keynesian unemployment or other types of short-run imbalances" [loc. cit., p. 4].

Grandmont, surveying these models, notes that the simple case in which prices are temporarily fixed in each period has been a fruitful approach to a host of issues:

> In particular it is possible to reach a temporary equilibrium where there is an excess supply both in the market for the output of the firms and in the labor market, that is, which displays Keynesian unemployment. Both these models are able to generate other situations as well; for instance, one in which there is an excess demand for output and an excess supply of labor (stagflation or classical unemployment), or one in which there is an excess demand in both markets (repressed inflation) [Grandmont, 1977, p. 55].

Grandmont's survey identifies a number of potential improvements and extensions of this type of analysis. We need better justifications for the expectational basis on which the traders generate trade offers, more realistic information flows and forecasts, a dynamic related to information changes, etc. His final opinion, though, is that such models "could provide a sound microeconomic foundation to macroeconomic theory" [ibid., p. 554].

Let us try to assess this claim.

A summing up

The work surveyed in this chapter has been guided by the persistent intuition of a number of theorists that the dynamics of general equilibrium theory, the disequilibrium stories that can be told in neo-Walrasian language, are extremely fictitious ones. The appalling scarcity of sensible adjustment-to-equilibrium fables reduces the hold that the usual microeconomic analysis should have over our analytic lives. As Leijonhufvud [1974] states, it is far from the case that "(*a*) microtheory is in good shape, (*b*) macrotheory is in rather bad shape, and (*c*) that it is up to macroeconomists to put the Humpty Dumpty of general economic theory together again by rebuilding their models with building-blocks that contemporary microeconomics provides" [p. 1].

To be brutal about the matter, any macroeconomist who relies on the rock-solid foundations of general disequilibrium theory to reconstruct macroeconomics has been misled by the technical sophistication of models which have weak conclusions.

The path through disequilibrium theory requires one to step through analytic time. It seems to require specific partial theories of how time intervals for particular decisions are cut up, then meshed together again. Agents have information from the "past" and expectations about the future. There are a few futures markets which link time periods, or assets which can be carried over period-to-period. Decisions are made, "mistakes" may be recognized, and incompatibilities between plans may or may not show up in the market. Such time-production sequences seem to involve money in essential ways. For Keynes, and monetary theory, money serves to link past, present, and future, and the desire to hold money is a measure of the distrust an agent has in the present about his ability *now* to coordinate his future plans.

In the disequilibrium stories told in this chapter, medium of exchange money appears to serve a coordinating function. A trader must allocate *now* some money to provide for future transactions. Such money "is probably indispensable [in models!] for the introduction of firms into the trading process ... [for] Without the introduction of money, firms would value their holdings the same whether or not they sold them" [Fisher, 1976, p. 15].

In a similar vein, Arrow and Hahn recognize that money is indispensable for these sequential models, and consequently there is a natural desire on the part of traders to reduce the flux of disappointment of expectations (and the lack of period-by-period coordination) by permitting money contracts. Indeed, "if a serious monetary theory comes to be written, the fact that contracts are . . . made in terms of money will be of considerable importance" [Arrow and Hahn, 1971, p. 357].

But, it must be recognized, as Hahn states, that "Money, in economic theory, always brings out the worst in us" [Hahn in Harcourt, 1977, p. 31].

It is not, in Hahn's view, any positive accomplishment of the Drèze–Benassy theory that the disequilibrium story is based on Clower's "money-buys-goods" approach. For Hahn, this is a "persistent false trail" for it is

> a muddle to suppose that in the absence of this axiomatic restriction, things would be any different. In reality there are many goods. In a barter world a man would not offer his labor in exchange for, say, some of the sulphuric acid he helps to produce except on the speculative basis that he could exchange it again. One would expect "market failure" to be far worse here than in an economy with a medium of exchange [ibid., p. 31].

The assumption that neo-Keynesian disequilibrium, a theory of short-side rationing really, bears any relation to Keynes is, for Hahn, a barbarism perpetrated by the French sons of Walras. In the Benassy model, for instance, "if the demand for shoes, before any quantity constraint is perceived, exceeds the supply of shoes then the demand side will be rationed . . . In Keynesian economics [on the other hand] suppliers of shoes lose inventories and demands are satisfied" [ibid., p. 36].

The critique outlined in Hahn's paper extends to the short-period fixed price assumption: it is "not that prices were fixed because agents think about price only on Mondays but because 'normal' price expectations combined with inventories prevented price from changing by much" [ibid., p. 36].

Despite those reservations, it is clear to critics like Hahn, Fisher, and Arrow that Keynesian theory cannot be easily reconstructed from the perfectly competitive stories of price adjustment. Whether or not an "auctioneer" is assumed, the tatonnement must be abandoned in any model directed to answering macroeconomic questions.

"Real-time" adjustment is badly handled in all these models. Benassy [1975] writes "Cependant la faiblesse majeure des théories présentées ici reste le caractère extrêmement limité des analyses stok-flux, notamment pour ce qui est de l'accumulation. Des progrès dans ce domaine permettraient de remplacer la périodisation abstraite des modèles par une analyse en 'temps réel' absolument nécessaire pour une application de ces modèles à la réalité."

In his recent survey of monetary theory, Stanley Fischer commented on these developments saying [1975, p. 161]: "While disequilibrium analysis has succeeded in presenting models in which many Keynesian notions—particularly that of effective demand—are clarified, it remains to be seen whether the same analytical structure will prove useful when applied to situations in which price determination is endogenous."

It is easy to agree with this call for methodological caution. It is not so easy, however, to continue telling macroeconomic stories that rely on a theory of general equilibrium dynamics abandoned over a decade ago by most serious investigators. The tatonnement cannot be considered a harmless "as if" assumption if it is logically inconsistent with other assumptions in the models we use.

8

Edgeworthian equilibrium

The last dozen years have seen a reformulation of general equilibrium theory in which "markets" and "market behavior" are pushed into the background while the acts of individual exchange are brought into sharper focus. This game-theoretic approach to microeconomics, whose progenitor was Edgeworth not Walras, is likewise important for the light it sheds on the microfoundations of macroeconomics. Although less well-developed than neo-Walrasian analysis, Edgeworthian models too can formulate at the disaggregated level a number of intrinsically macroeconomic concerns. To see this, however, it is necessary to develop some of the conceptual framework, since it is by no means as widely utilized, or taught, by economists as is neo-Walrasianism.

One begins by specifying a given set of economic agents, called traders (T), such that each trader has a well-behaved preference ordering over goods bundles [see Weintraub, 1975]. Thus, for trader $t \in T$, there exists a relation $\precsim_t$ satisfying transitivity, connectedness, continuity, semi-strict convexity, and non-satiation.

Define a coalition of traders as a subset $S \subset T$, and identify goods bundles with vectors $x \in R_+^n$, the non-negative orthant of Euclidean n-space. In an exchange model, let x_t^0 represent the initial bundle held by trader $t \in T$. An allocation is an assignment of a bundle to each trader, so that if x_t is a bundle, $x = \underset{t \in T}{X} x_t$ is an allocation, where X is the Cartesian product.

Using this terminology, an allocation x is feasible for coalition S if

$$\sum_{s \in S} x_s \leq \sum_{s \in S} x_s^o \tag{1}$$

that is, an allocation is feasible for a set of traders if they can achieve it without exceeding the resources held initially by the coalition—it can thus be obtained by a redistribution.

Consider the concept of equilibrium. For a neo-Walrasian model, this suggests the possibility that markets can pre-reconcile individual choices. In an Edgeworthian framework, however, we are concerned not with markets but with acts of individual exchange. As an equilibrium concept we need some logical rest-point of an exchange mechanism. If it is possible for two individuals to gain from trade, that pre-trade allocation ought not to be termed an equilibrium. Intuitively, equilibrium will occur when no traders can improve their positions by exchange. The implications of this notion will be explored shortly, but we formalize this by saying that an allocation x is *dominated* (or blocked) via coalition S if there exists a feasible allocation for S, x' say, with $x_s \prec_s x_s'$ for all $s \in S$. That is, an allocation which each strictly prefers and which is achievable by them by redistribution of their initial resources.

The *core* of the (exchange) economy is defined as the set of all allocations that are feasible and undominated via any coalition. The language has a picturesque interpretation. Think of the set of all feasible allocations as a big convex set (an apple) in the plane. For a three trader economy, there are $2^3 - 1 = 7$ non-null coalitions, of which three consist only of single trader coalitions which cannot be involved in exchange. There are thus four possible "trading" coalitions: the three two-person subsets, and the one three-person subset. Consider the first two-person coalition. If it dominates any feasible allocations, those which it dominates are removed, or sliced off, from the set of feasible allocations. Continue this procedure for each trading coalition, so each cuts a slice from the initial feasible set. What is left of the set at the end of this finite algorithm is the set of allocations undominated via any coalition, and it will "look like" the core of a sliced apple.

Core allocations are Pareto-efficient. To see this, consider the coalition consisting of all traders. Since no other allocation dominates the core allocation via the coalition of all traders, this means that any core allocation is such that at least one trader would be worse off at a non-core feasible allocation. It is, of course, possible for a Pareto-efficient allocation to be outside the core.

To cast these arguments in a more familiar context, it may be advantageous to recall the two-person, two-commodity exchange problem represented by an Edgeworth–Bowley box diagram. Locate the initial endowment point at the northwest corner as in Fig. 8.1, with origins for traders A and B at O_A and O_B. Measure amounts of good 1 horizontally and good 2 vertically. The indifference curves for A and B, which pass through the initial endowment i, are labelled I_A and I_B, and the tangencies between the indifference maps trace out the contract curve, C. Every point in the box diagram is a feasible allocation, since all are attainable by redistributions. It should be clear that the portion of C which does not lie below I_A or above I_B is the core, since it consists of those allocations that no coalition (the coalitions are A, B, and (A,B)) finds more desirable and can, in fact, effect.

It is thus easy to see that in this example (1) the core is a subset of the set of Pareto-efficient allocations; (2) for any price system such that trade takes place, the competitive allocation with respect to that price system is in the core; and (3) if both traders have identical preferences (and hence identical utility indicators), the allocation that gives equal utility shares to each of the traders is in the core.

> Suppose now that a third household [trader] enters the economy. New possibilities of bargaining and, therefore, of blocking arise from the two-member coalitions. Thus, a proposed allocation is blocked not merely if any one household is driven below its endowment level, but also if any two members can jointly improve their lots by trades that do not involve the third. This suggests that in some

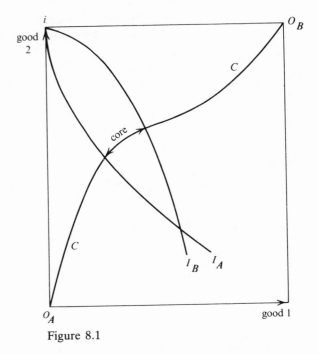

Figure 8.1

sense the range of unblocked allocations becomes smaller when there are more households [Arrow and Hahn, 1971, p. 185].

This argument was explored, though not generally established, by Edgeworth. He suggested that as the number of traders increased, i.e., as the economy became more perfectly competitive, the range of potential trading outcomes—equilibrium allocations—approached, in the limit, the competitive equilibrium allocation. The formalization and rigorous proof of Edgeworth's conjecture has been a major contribution of economic theory. The result has meant that new approaches to the study of systemic coordination are possible.

Competitive equilibrium and the core

It is not difficult to show that, for exchange economies, if (p^*, x^*) is a competitive equilibrium, then x^* is in the core. For suppose x^* is non-core. Then x^* is dominated (via some coalition S) by an allocation x^1 such that, for x_s^0 the initial bundle held by trader s,

$$\sum_{s \in S} x_s^1 \leqslant \sum_{s \in S} x_s^0 \tag{2}$$

and

$$x_s^1 \succ_s x_s^* \text{ for all } s \in S \tag{3}$$

But since a competitive equilibrium allocation is the best among all allocations which can be purchased at the equilibrium price vector, we have

$$x_s^* \succsim_s x_s \text{ if } p^* x_s < p^* x_s^0 \text{ for all } s \in S \tag{4}$$

From (3), then,

$$p^* x_s^1 > p^* x_s^0 \text{ for all } s \in S \tag{5}$$

and thus

$$\sum_{s \in S} p^* x_s^1 > \sum_{s \in S} p^* x_s^0 \tag{6}$$

But since $p^* > 0$, multiplying equation (2) by p^* yields

$$\sum_{s \in S} p^* x_s^1 \leqslant \sum_{s \in S} p^* x_s^0 \tag{7}$$

The contradiction between (6) and (7) entails that the supposition that x^* was non-core must be abandoned. *Thus competitive allocations are core allocations.*

The converse of this theorem would say that every core allocation is a competitive equilibrium. In general, though, this is false. It is, however, true that:

> for each pair consisting of an economy and an unblocked allocation for it, we can choose a price vector so that allocation approximately satisfies the conditions for a compensated equilibrium . . . [and] it is asserted that the *average* discrepancy from equilibrium is a number that is inversely proportional to the size of the economy [i.e., the number of traders] and therefore approaches zero for large economies [Arrow and Hahn, 1971, p. 191].

As the number of traders in an exchange economy increases, the core "shrinks" to a limit, the set of competitive allocations. If we model the economy *ab initio* with an uncountably infinite set of traders (each trader indexed, say, by a point in the interval (0,1)) then the core coincides with the competitive allocations for the model [Aumann, 1964].

The importance of these results should not be lost through either understatement or technical opaqueness. The conceptual framework which underlies the construction is definitely not neo-Walrasian, yet the results have much to contribute to an understanding of the mental experiments which structure micro-economic reasoning.

In the neo-Walrasian system, coordinated outcomes were assured when markets served to disseminate the information about the reconcilability of plans of the agents: market price was a signal to agents to initiate revisions of buy and sell orders. This conception required a central auctioneer, or planning agency *cum* computer, to generate those signals since the agents never formally met to effect exchanges. All planned transactions were communicated to the auctioneer, and all effective transactions costs were hidden under the dias on which the auctioneer stood.

Without a central market, and market maker, one is left with agents attempting to make themselves better off through trade. The process involves inter-agent communication, tentative offers, contracting, re-contracting, and transacting. There is no information center, no one but other similar agents to whom a given agent can turn.

Consequently the neo-Walrasian model appears "rigged" to induce coordination success, at least when compared to the Edgeworthian schema. It was argued in Chapter 5 that the basic problems of macroeconomics are related to systems that exhibit coordination failures with alarming regularity. The Edgeworth model, with its lack of a central coordinator, thus may be well-suited to the posing of macroeconomic questions. Since equilibria in Edgeworth models are, under some circumstances and arrangements, competitive equilibria of related neo-Walrasian systems, Edgeworth models can be linked to systems that produce coordination successes. The Edgeworth model thus seems to hold out some promise of being able to capture the essence of Leijonhufvud's "corridor" behavior. It is a general equilibrium system that sometimes coordinates activity well and sometimes coordinates activity badly. For this reason the Edgeworth model may have something important to add to the question of "what is an appropriate microfoundation for macroeconomics?"

It should be noted, before we proceed, that macroeconomics has not been on the research agenda for most "core" theorists. Their work has generalized and extended the exchange model to economies permitting production, public goods, externalities, monopoly, and oligopoly (see Volker Boehm [1974]). The work has concentrated on basic microeconomics, and has tended to show satisfying unities in the structure of economic theory. Arrow's Impossibility Theorem, external diseconomies, and public goods problems can all be linked to the failure of some structurally similar games to possess a core (see William H. Riker and Peter C. Ordeshook [1972] and Robert Wilson [1973]). Since core allocations are produced by the Invisible Hand, their nonexistence and "market failures" are inextricably linked.

It is to the area of model selection, and model structure, that we must turn in order to assay the usefulness of Edgeworthian analysis. We must be careful, though, to keep statics and dynamics separate. The core is an equilibrium concept, since it is an allocation that, once reached, will not be modified. Any modification requires a trading coalition to form and improve the given allocation. The core seems to embody a costless recontracting mechanism run either by a benevolent auctioneer, a deity who forms trading coalitions, or chance. There is not, however, any notion of time involved in this process. There is not even the economic quick-time of a Walrasian tatonnement, since there is no explicit market experiment being performed.

Recontracting in notional time
The economics of Edgeworthian models relies on modes

of questioning that do not usually appear in neo-Walrasian logic. We need to make behavioral assumptions about the exchange process, about coalition formation, and about the information structure of particular realizations of trading economies. One specific set of arrangements is based on the conceptual experiment of recontracting designed by Edgeworth.

Suppose we have an exchange economy and the core associated with it. As Feldman sees it,

> Recontracting is a process of proposal, challenge, and counter-proposal, in which no exchanges are actually made outside the core. At each stage of the process an allocation of good or utilities is put before the economy. If some group of traders finds that it can do better on its own, it challenges or blocks the proposal. It then proposes an alternative allocation, which it prefers, and which it can somehow achieve by itself, but which may make its non-members worse off than they were before [Feldman, 1974, p. 35].

As Green notes, the formalization of any recontract scheme must directly face three major questions:

> (i) If several blocking coalitions are possible [at some stage of the process] . . . which one actually forms and proposes the blocking allocation?
> (ii) In general . . . there will be many allocations . . . superior to [the suggested one] . . . which of these will actually be chosen . . . to form the blocking allocation?
> (iii) . . . What allocation is given to the people not in [the blocking coalition] . . .? [Green, 1974, p. 22]

When phrased in this manner, the information dissemination process determines the outcome. Prices, and price changes, are market phenomena and in their absence their information–theoretic properties must be reintroduced by other constructions.

A formal recontract model is given by a set of assumptions which answer the questions (i)–(iii) above. Consider the set of blocking coalitions that dominate a given proposal. (If such did not exist, the proposed allocation would be core, and the process would stop.) Green assumes that for each collection of possible blocking coalitions, "there is a strictly positive probability distribution that determines which coalition will, in fact, block the current proposal" [ibid., p. 24]. Intuitively, the potential blocking coalition must exchange information "faster" than all rival coalitions. If all traders are thought of as milling about in a large room with no auctioneer, trading begins with the implicit suggested allocation of "initial holdings to everyone." As traders move around and talk (exchange information about preferences, desired trades, and initial resources), one coalition is the first to form and announce "We can do better for ourselves." That allocation is announced by one of the group members to the assemblage, who now mill about to try to find a coalition to block that allocation, etc.

If a coalition could block a given suggested allocation x with an allocation y, and if ε is a vector of *small* positive numbers, it might be possible for it to have blocked with $y + \varepsilon$, or even $y - \varepsilon$. Green assumes that the blocking coalition, S, possesses sufficient information to choose a Pareto-efficient allocation (relative to S) as the blocking allocation. In answer to question (iii), Green assumes that traders left out of the given blocking coalition select a point in the set of Pareto-efficient allocations available to the coalition of all excluded traders (the coalition complementary to S), although this is not necessarily as good an outcome for them as was the original—and now blocked by S—proposal.

Green's assumptions thus "generate a sequence of proposals (allocations) $\{x_t\}$ beginning from an arbitrary x_0 such that for each t there exists a coalition S_t such that S_t blocks x_{t-1}" [p. 22]. The theorem that emerges states "Let x_0 be an arbitrary proposal. Then the probability that x_t is not in the core approaches zero with t" [Green, 1974, p. 22].

Feldman's analysis of the recontract mechanism is similar to Green's but provides additional insight into the underlying differences between market oriented neo-Walrasianism and the exchange emphasis of Edgworthian models. For Feldman, [1974] a proposal is a utility vector. A partially specified recontracting process (p.s.r.p.) begins with a proposal which is a feasible (attainable) utility vector for the set of traders N. Somehow a coalition $S \subset N$ is chosen. Examine all utility allocations that are attainable by S and that block the initial proposal. If such exist, choose one. If such do not exist, keep the initial allocation. This is one iteration of the p.s.r.p. The p.s.r.p. continues with repeated (perhaps an infinite number of) iterations.

Feldman proves that under reasonable assumptions about utility allocations, and the assumption that the set of S-attainable utility allocations is *finite*, the p.s.r.p. is stable if and only if the core is non-empty. Stability here means that one can reach a core vector via the process in a finite number of steps.

In order to tell more interesting stories we need to specify (a) how an initial proposal is generated, (b) how a blocking coalition forms, (c) how that coalition chooses its blocking allocation, and (d) how other traders react. Feldman introduces the random recontracting process [1973] to generate the p.s.r.p. as follows: each utility vector for N is assigned a positive probability, and similarly each utility vector attainable by $S \subset N$ is assigned a positive probability p_q. Then if proposal x_i is suggested, choose a coalition according to its probability. That is, if S_q blocks x_i choose x_j out of the set of allocations for S_q which block x_i by the conditional probability

$$\hat{p}_j / \sum_m \hat{p}_m$$

where the index m runs over all allocations which block x_i via the coalition S_q. If S_q cannot block, stay at x_i. This is one iteration. For the process Feldman established convergence (with probability one) to the core in a finite number of steps.

The major differences between Feldman's and Green's results, apart from the finiteness assumption, can be related to Green's questions (ii) and (iii). Green assumes "that the blocking coalition is assigned a utility vector which is Pareto optimal for it and the complement of the blocking coalition is also assigned a Pareto optimal utility vector ... [Feldman assumes] that the blocking coalition is assigned a blocking utility vector which need not be Pareto optimal, and its complement is assigned a 'no-trade' utility vector" [Feldman, 1974, p. 41].

A theory of money and financial institutions

We have examined these papers in some detail primarily because they illustrate the non-Walrasian focus of Edgeworth models. The unsettled areas, where one has to take extreme care with the assumptions and model specification, are precisely in those areas of information content and inter-agent communication which are swept aside in neo-Walrasian systems which postulate the existence of markets and an auctioneer.

Martin Shubik, one of the originators of current applications of game theory to economics, is currently developing a non-Walrasian approach to general equilibrium theory specifically directed at macro-monetary theory concerns.[1]

He argues that the discipline imposed by the use of game theoretic modelling techniques requires complete specification of strategies, rules, payoffs, and institutions. Consequently the descriptive structure is closer to real agents and modern institutions than is the neo-Walrasian theory. He notes, for example, that

> When a system is in equilibrium and there is no uncertainty most of the reasons for money and financial institutions disappear. Thus to start with a general equilibrium [ADM] framework to study the role of money and financial institutions is to throw most of the problem away. What remains is a safe and mildly interesting set of problems for mathematical economists concerning the combinatorics of barter and transactions costs [Shubik, 1975, p. 552].

Shubik specifically rejects the core as an appropriate solution concept since it is a "cooperative" equilibrium requiring action (coalition formation) in recognition of potential mutual gain. For Shubik, this precludes the observed non-cooperative structure of unrestrained agent choice. Cooperation, if it exists, is better

[1] Shubik's unpublished book is titled "The Theory of Money and Financial Institutions." Various chapters, denoted by roman numerals, have appeared as Cowles Foundation Discussion papers at Yale University. See also [Shubik, 1975].

thought of as something induced by the institutional environment in which the agent lives. The simple closed economic system is thus initially modelled as a non-cooperative n-person game.

Into this framework Shubik introduces commodity money (III) and fiat money (V). Complexity is developed with three "limiting" processes. That is, the model is extended to a larger number of competitors (XXXV), a longer time horizon (XXXIV), and more sophisticated information systems (XXXIII).

The monetary theory that is developed provides an interesting link between microeconomics and macroeconomics. Expectations, forecasting, and control are all developed by considering agent strategies which are worked out in an integrated monetary system. Fiat money, for example, acts as a form of insurance or generalized future contract (V). If the money supply is fixed, hoarding may take place even with an infinite number of competitors (VI).

A number of other traditional topics may be broached in the non-cooperative game structure. Transactions costs (VIII), uncertainty (XII), insurance (XVI), and banking (XIII) make natural appearances. The flavor of the model may be seen in a discrete-time setting where Shubik sets up (XXI) a trading economy which satisfies conditions sufficient to guarantee existence of a competitive equilibrium. In this case there exist two trading economies, one with bank money and one with both bank and fiat money, such that the money rate of interest is zero in the first and positive in the second. Thus a positive interest rate depends on an economy's having two types of money. (There is also a continuous-time version of this result (XXIII).)

Finally, the distribution and quantity of commodity money is critical in the proof that the non-cooperative equilibrium converges to the competitive equilibrium as the number of traders increases. Thus bankruptcy and credit problems are obviated when each trader has "enough" commodity money. In several papers Shubik examined the bankruptcy rules as institutional devices to guide the economy to a particular equilibrium (XXX, XXIV, XXXV).

We can thus see, in Shubik's work, that a number of microfoundations type concerns may be well-posed in an Edgeworthian framework. Although it is too early to evaluate the impact of such ideas, one may be confident that such approaches will attract the interest of many theorists in the years ahead.

Model selection

Since the core provides an alternative characterization of the competitive equilibrium, assumptions that guarantee existence of a core simultaneously establish equilibrium in the related Walrasian system. Put negatively, factors that inhibit coalition formation and cooperative inter-agent behavior may preclude the existence of a core; consequently the related Walrasian system might not exhibit coherent and coordinated outcomes. To the extent that macroeconomics is concerned with coordination failures, there is value in the study of microeconomic systems that call attention to behaviors and institutions that may produce those failures.

Studying the manner in which the Walrasian system might fail to produce coherent market outcomes provides few clues to the individual behaviors that generate the difficulties, since the Walrasian structure coordinates activity at the level of markets. The Edgeworth structure, however, gives prominence to inter-agent behavior. Problems involving imperfect information, uncertainty, unrealized expectations, and transactions constraints can be posed naturally in the model. Further, since it is this set of problems that restricts coalition behavior (and can entail the non-existence of core allocations), coordination failures can be linked directly to Keynesian concerns about uncertainty and expectations.

In the next chapter, then, we shall examine the behavior of Edgeworthian models in a dynamic setting and pose questions about the possibility of disequilibrium adjustment. We shall see that the transactions and information structures determine whether the models coordinate activity well or ill. The role of the medium of exchange money can thus be highlighted.

9

Edgeworth disequilibrium analysis

There is an analogue, for Edgeworth models, to disequilibrium analysis in Walrasian models. Instead of examining the market price adjustment mechanism, one could examine the patterns of exchange that individual traders create and face when required to complete transactions out of equilibrium. If the Walrasian framework is a model of how the institutions of a competitive market serve to organize and stabilize economic activity, then the Edgeworth system, which abstracts from the price mechanism, may appear as neoinstitutionalism.

There are two distinct themes to this literature: (1) problems of coordination, of resource allocation proper, in systems without competitive markets or (2) problems of monetary theory, like the role of money in a dynamic exchange setting.

In this chapter we will examine how disequilibrium trading models can generate systemic coordination successes and failures. This family of models has something to contribute to the microfoundations of macroeconomics literature. It is possible to design institutional arrangements for the conduct of disequilibrium activity in such a way that, under one set of arrangements, trading activity leads to coherent outcomes, but under alternative structures, coordination failures abound. We can formalize the role of the medium of exchange money as a systemic coordinator and identify its place among alternative transactions facilitators.

Before we proceed, however, we must note one terminological muddle. In many surveys and discussions, "Edgeworth process" refers to a disequilibrium adjustment mechanism which utilizes a variant of the tatonnement in which there are two state variables, prices and individual stocks of commodities. There are two adjustment mechanisms. One changes prices in the direction of excess demands, where those demands are now also functions of individual stocks. In the other, stocks change via trade when trade would increase the utility of the participants. Since this process was first examined by Uzawa [1962], who termed it an "Edgeworth Barter Process," the name has stuck although the work discussed in Chapter 8 shows that the Edgeworth recontract argument is better thought of as an exchange process, not a market price adjustment mechanism. In this sense the Uzawa paper is one in the family of (the equally misnamed) non-tatonnement processes discussed in Chapter 7.

Decentralized adjustment mechanisms

Without a centralized market or auctioneer to transmit price information, we become interested in how agents behave and change their decisions when their various plans are irreconcilable. In particular, we must examine how information is processed by the various agents. An information-decentralized process is one in which the signals transmitted by an agent convey information only about that agent. Exchange is decentralized when the agents act individualistically for gain, and not anonymously through markets.

One such mechanism, called the B-process (for "Bidding") was investigated by Hurwicz, Radner, and Reiter [1975]. For pure exchange with divisible commodities, the B process may be represented in an Edgeworth box diagram.

Each of participants one and two has an indifference curve I_1^0, I_2^0, passing through the initial endowment point i^0. The intersection of the two "better" sets forms the admissible trade region:

> The participant ... picks, according to an appropriate
> probability distribution, a trade, the *central bid*, from
> among those not inferior to his current endowment ...

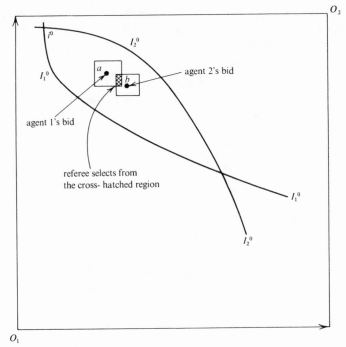

Figure 9.1

[But] he conveys not merely this central bid, but also—as alternatives—all trades within a specified "distance" from the central bid that are not inferior to the present endowment. Because the bids . . . contain a continuum of alternatives, the referee may be faced with a multiplicity of compatible bid combinations. He will then pick one of them at random to serve as the basis for trades to take place [Hurwicz, Radner, Reiter, 1975, p. 192].

Since trades take place while the process continues over time, at least in the pure exchange case, the B-process is a disequilibrium process. Since traders need only to generate information in a neighborhood of their endowment points, they need not provide information about their attitudes to trades which are very different from those which generated their current endowment. The information requirements for the agents in this model seem quite reasonable. The fact that trader utility is monotone-increasing throughout the process (and the convergence which can be shown for the sequence of bids) ensures that "the B-process is Pareto satisfactory and stochastically convergent to an optimum in most cases in which the perfectly competitive [tatonnement] process is Pareto satisfactory and stable" [ibid., p. 195].

Adjustment mechanisms like the B-process do not begin with a competitive equilibrium and examine how the market realizes that state. Instead, one simply asks whether the terminal points of particular dynamic processes have any "nice" properties: "Viewed in computational terms, processes such as the competitive mechanism 'print out' the final (equilibrium) result—if and when reached—and stop; others, like the B-process, continue searching for a better solution indefinitely, but when in equilibrium keep 'printing out' the answer already found" [ibid., p. 189].

The major difficulty with competitive processes is that there is no way to assure *any* coherent outcome before the terminal state is reached. In a tatonnement trade is precluded out-of-equilibrium and adjustment takes place in virtual (auctioneer) time to preclude real time decision costs.

In abandoning this approach we must work with ongoing, actual time processes. We must continually ask about the compatibility of plans prior to terminal states, institutions which mitigate the costs of disequilibrium activity, incentives, signals, transactions rules and the like. For example, "it is not obvious that the traders won't 'get stuck' at some nonoptional position, in which case the process would be wasteful" [Hurwicz, 1973, p. 21].

Surveying such models in 1973, Hurwicz broached the tentative conclusion: "The new mechanisms are somewhat like synthetic chemicals: even if not usable for practical purposes, they can be studied in a pure form and so contribute to our understanding of the difficulties and potentialities of design" [ibid., p. 27].

This self-consciously design-oriented point of view is a natural context for work in microfoundations of macroeconomics. A neo-Walrasian competitive equilibrium "hides" the difficulties of time and coordination behind the construction of a pre-existing market. Edgeworthian disequilibrium analysis exhibits those difficulties for all to see. It directs attention to ways in which real institutions function to coordinate inharmonious choice.

Convergence to Pareto outcomes

A particularly simple process of this type may serve to direct attention to those monetary theoretic themes which are currently having a lively rebirth when joined to this Edgeworthian family of models [Graham and Weintraub, 1975].

Recalling the Green and Feldman discussions of recontracting in the previous chapter, consider a general equilibrium system of n goods and a finite set of traders, called T. Suppose each trader, t, has the usual preference structure, $\precsim_t$, on goods vectors $x \in R_+^n$, and begins with an endowment i_t^0, so that the initial allocation is $i0 \in \underset{T}{X} i_t^0$. Let the aggregate of goods be denoted by I, so that $I = \underset{T}{\sum} i_t^0$.

Define a trading process as follows: if the initial allocation is not Pareto-efficient, there will be a set of coalitions and their corresponding allocations which could dominate or block i^0. Suppose one such coalition forms, and trade takes place. If this new allocation is Pareto-efficient, the process stops. If it is not, the process iterates. This process defines a blocking sequence where, at the nth iteration,

$$i_t^n = x_t^n \quad \text{if } t \in S^n \text{ or} \tag{*}$$

$$i_t^n = i_t^{n-1} \quad \text{if } t \in T - S^n$$

if, given i^{n-1}, x^n blocks i^{n-1} via $S^n \subset T$.

Intuitively, for a non-Pareto allocation, many coalitions could gain from trade. Let one coalition form and gain, and let those traders *not* in the coalition keep what they have. Examine the new allocation, and repeat the argument. Does this process have a terminal state (a "final" allocation) and, if so, what are its properties?

Even though this process, unlike recontracting, takes place in real time and involves trade prior to the reconciliation of plans, certain questions about coalition formation and choice of allocation must be faced directly. The questions Green raised about which coalitions form, which trades they will seek, and what happens to non-included traders in fact are more naturally considered in this disequilibrium context. In virtual or recontract time, if imperfect information is the only barrier to coalition formation, one should simply allow the coalitions to search longer for better information. Since the major cost of that information search is the opportunity cost of the agent's time, a model which works in virtual time has only artificial barriers to the realization of a state of perfect information. It is costly to waste real time. Auctioneer time is cheap.

The core is no longer a possible terminal state. The core, recall, depended on initial endowments. In a disequilibrium exchange process those endowments change at each iteration. A final allocation, if reached at the nth iteration, is "core" with respect to the endowments at the $(n-1)$th iteration, but this property is of little interest since it does not help characterize the sequence of allocations that the process generates.

Returning to Green's questions, it should be clear that information and transactions costs do play a major role in generating blocking sequences over real (iteration) time. If either contact (information) costs to potential coalition members or contract ("physical" transaction or exchange) costs to blocking coalition members are very large, then no trade will take place and the sequence terminates at the initial allocation. If these costs are zero, we should reach a Pareto-efficient terminal state in which no agents could gain from trade. These arguments can be seen geometrically in the case of two goods.

Let P^n be the aggregate better set[1] associated with the allocation that arises from the nth iteration of the process. Formally,

$$P^n = \left\{ \sum_T x_t^n : x_t^n \succsim_t i_t^{n-1} \text{ all } t \in T \right\}.$$

---

[1] That is, the set of bundles summed over all traders which leaves each trader at least as well off as he was with his original bundle.

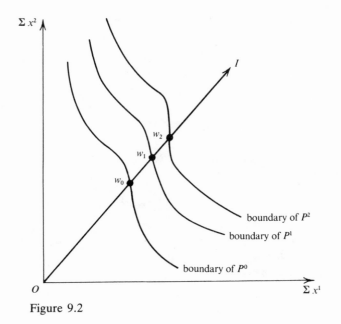

Figure 9.2

Certainly $P^0 \supseteq P^1 \supseteq P^2 \supseteq \ldots P^n \supseteq \ldots$

We represent these sets, and I which is the aggregate intial bundle, in Fig. 9.2 [see Graham, Jacobson, Weintraub, 1972].

If we draw a line from the origin to I, and note the intersections of this line with the (lower) boundaries of the P^n sets, we can "pick off" a sequence of points $\{w_n\}$ which represent the smallest endowment *in the proportions of I* that belongs to the aggregate preferred set corresponding to the allocation i^n. $\{w_n\}$ is a non-decreasing sequence on the closed unit interval, for if the boundary of P^n goes through I, then $w^n = 1$. $1 - w_n$ measures the potential gain from trade remaining after n iterations of the trading process.

Now as the interation pushes a P^n sufficiently northeast so that I is on the boundary of a particular P^n, no more trade will take place, and the allocation which generated P^n will be Pareto-efficient. In terms of the $\{w_n\}$ sequence there are no further gains from trade possible if $\lim_{n}\{w_n\} = 1$. How can this fail to occur? The only real problem would involve convergence of $\{w_n\}$ (and the P^n sets) to some $v < 1$, so the P^n sets "bunch up" before they reach I. This would mean that the potential gain from trade measured by $1-v$ is forever unrealized. This should not happen in a world of costless information because traders there could costlessly improve their allocation. We are thus led to postulate a costless intercommunication assumption in the form "the probability of no further trade, given an allocation that is not Pareto, is zero." In technical language assume that "for all $\varepsilon > 0$ there exists $\delta > 0$ such that

$$\text{prob} \left[1-w_{n+1} > (1 - \delta)(1-w_n)\right] < \varepsilon \quad \text{for all } n."$$

With this assumption, it can be shown that $\{w_n\}$ converges to 1 with probability one, so the blocking sequence defined by (*) converges to a Pareto-efficient allocation with probability one.

In the presence of real transactions costs, resources are used up in every iteration. In terms of the diagram, I does not remain fixed, but rather it moves generally southwest at every iteration as I, I^1, I^2, ... We specify $c = \min_{n}\{\| I^n - I^{n+1}\|\}$, or that real resources in the amount $c > 0$ must be expended to contract for any trade.

For the process (*) described above, it is not hard to see that after a finite number of iterations, say $\bar{n}$, $I^{\bar{n}}$ is within distance c of the boundary of P^n, and so i^n is a Pareto-allocation. In terms of the $\{w_n\}$ sequence, at each successive iteration some fraction of the potential gains from trade are dissipated through the physical act of exchange (perhaps interpreted by the time it takes to physically redistribute commodities).

The lessons to be drawn from these models are reminiscent of Adam Smith. As Feldman states: "An invisible hand (self-interest) pushes an economy to optimality in the sense of Pareto, even if the 'push' is a sequence of random shoves rather than a sequence of market price adjustments" [Feldman, 1974, p. 43].

What, then, disturbs the smooth functioning of these processes as they lead inexorably coordinated outcomes? In decentralized trading, the clue is provided by the necessity of our specifying that there exists costless information and costless trading. In actual economies, where such costs exist, we have institutions like money and markets to reduce the cost of barter exchange. To link these simple models of convergence to Pareto allocations to the micro-foundations literature on money and exchange, we must thus examine the exchange mechanism a bit more closely.

Bilateral versus multilateral exchange

The processes embedded in Edgeworthian disequilibrium models are derived from coalition formation. If there are barriers to such formation, it is unlikely that terminal states of the process will induce coordinated outcomes. Costly information is thus central since large coalitions are more costly to form than small ones. But what if the only Pareto improving trade for society at the nth iteration were to involve the coalition of all traders passing all their goods to the trader on their right? Such a case, though conceivable, would be awkward. As F. Fisher notes,

> it is possible that there is no mutually advantageous bilateral or trilateral or quadrilateral trade and that the only mutually advantageous trade involves a very complicated swapping of commodites among millions of people. To require, as the Edgeworth process does, that such a trade must take place is to put very heavy requirements on the dissemination of information and to assume away the costs of coalition formation" [Fisher, 1976, p. 12].

We can rephrase this concern by asking whether, for a given blocking sequence which terminates in a Pareto-efficient alloca-tion, it is possible to find another blocking sequence involving coalitions of smaller size at each iteration? In the best of cases we seek a sequence of bilateral trades that lead to a Pareto-allocation via the Edgeworth (*) process.

In a [1968] paper, Rader considered this question of pairwise Pareto optimality, or allocations which cannot be improved upon by bilateral trade. He was able to show that if there was a trader who could deal in all commodities under a given pairwise optimal allocation, then that allocation would be (overall) Pareto optimal.

Thus in economies where multilateral trade is prohibitively expensive, a broker or middleman could effect the efficient outcome.

The role of the broker is to induce all trades to take place in a single "trading stall." If there are three traders, there are $2^3 - 1 - 3 = 4$ possible trading groups. Introducing a broker, there are exactly three trading groups if all trades are bilateral with the broker. The problem is that complicated commodity swaps might need big coalitions. This leads naturally to the observation that if one requires that goods trade not against goods but only against money, those complicated commodity exchanges could be broken down into a sequence of simpler goods–money exchanges perhaps requiring smaller coalitions.

Feldman established that this was indeed the case. He proved that:

> under fairly general conditions, a pairwise optimal allocation is Pareto optimal if it assigns each trader a positive quantity of one good (which we will call "money"), for which each trader has a positive marginal utility. As a corollary . . . certain types of sequences of bilateral trades will always carry an economy to its set of Pareto optimal allocations [Feldman, 1973a, p. 463].

Strictly convex preferences were necessary for the results. The role of money, or "partial" money, is *not* that of a transactions cost minimizing device. It is rather an information cost minimizer in the sense that money permits the realization of cheap (bilateral rather than multilateral) sequences which reach Pareto allocations. This result is a strong one, and holds "even though there are no markets, no well-defined prices, traders are completely ignorant of possible future exchange ratios, and they are dreadfully conservative in the sense that they make no trades which do not directly and immediately gratify them" [Feldman, 1973a, p. 471].

The Rader and Feldman papers adopted a point of view akin to the assertion that multilateral trade is infinitely costly while bilateral trade is costless. It is thus natural to ask whether coalitions of size greater than two, but less than m = number of traders in the economy, could also generate trading sequences which converge to Pareto allocations.

A paper by Paul Madden [1975] examined this problem in a (*) model with n commodities and m traders. Call an allocation l-way Pareto efficient when for all trading coalitions of size l, the allocation is feasible and undominated via any coalition of size l or less (e.g., pairwise Pareto optimality is 2-wise, etc.). Maddan showed that, if utility is semi-strictly quasi-concave, l-way Pareto efficiency implies overall Pareto efficiency if $l \geqslant n + 1$. If, in addition, utility is continuous, and traders are non-satiated, then the result can be strengthened to $l > n$.

Further, Madden proved convergence theorems for "large" coalitions using, not (*), but a process which involved traders' meeting in groups of given size in a cyclic fashion. This process is a special case of (*), and for it Madden established overall Pareto efficiency. The resulting "size" theorems showed that it is thus possible to achieve convergence using coalitions of size $n + 1$ where n is the number of commodities.

In a related paper, Graham, Peterson, Jennergren and Weintraub [1976] established that, "under a simple free disposal assumption of the type suggested by Madden ... if a mutually advantageous trade is possible (among all traders) it is possible among m or fewer traders (where m = number of commodities)" [loc. cit., p. 443]. Further, using the (*) process directly, it was shown that even if barter groups are restricted to coalitions of size m, the limit points of the process are Pareto efficient.

The overall import of these results has been questioned by Fisher who suggests that "such [results do] not really get out of the difficulty [i.e., costs of forming large coalitions], especially when commodities at different dates are counted as different commodities" [Fisher, 1976, p. 27, n. 14]. This remark seems to miss the point. It is not that the Edgeworth disequilibrium process is considered to be a realistic mechanism for actual economies, but rather it is a framework for posing those questions about decentralization of exchange, barter inefficiency, and the difficulties that an institution-free economy has in generating coordinated outcomes. The lessons are those of Feldman's that money-like commodities are vitally important if coordination is induced by bilateral activity, or Rader's that a broker or broker substitute is needed to generate market exchange results that correspond to the behavior of actual exchange processes.

More interesting are the microfoundations desiderata embedded in this exchange process. As exchange money plays a co-ordinating role, there is a legitimate context for various monetary theoretic themes without having to introduce neo-Walrasian markets or price adjustment subsystems. For this reason, these Edgeworth disequilibrium process results have been incorporated into areas of macroeconomics which are particularly unsettled and quite intractable to neo-Walrasian reasoning; it is to such matters that we now turn.

Money and exchange
In their [1975] *Econometrica* paper, Ostroy and Starr examined bilateral exchange with and without money and, for the Edgeworthian disequilibrium process framework, were able to phrase answers to a number of older questions about the inefficiency of barter and the relevant differences between exchange and monetary systems. They showed that, in bilateral trade sequences constrained by reasonable trading rules for *given price ratios of goods,* the only *decentralized* processes that lead sequences to the equilibrium involve money.

In some ways, this framework is a curious amalgam of neo-Walrasian analysis (equilibrium prices must come from a market, or meta-model conceptual experiment) and disequilibrium trading dynamics. As Weber [1977] notes, Ostroy and Starr

> introduce money into the model as a bookkeeping entry at a central monetary authority . . . The role of money . . . is to make up the difference in value between [an agent's] sales and receipts in a form which is acceptable to both parties to the transaction. At the beginning and end of any trading period all agents will have zero balances at the monetary authority [Weber, 1977, p. 8].

This arrangement forces the view that "money will be used

because of *means of payment uncertainty* . . . [Further,] what will become and be used as money is not necessarily connected with the physical characteristics of money . . . [so] that money can be an institution" [ibid., p. 9].

The Ostroy–Starr paper provides a particularly elegant example of the interplay between exchange dynamics and monetary theory. Such work in the microfoundations of money was criticized by Fischer who concluded:

> This work is obviously both difficult and only at a beginning. It is not clear where, if anywhere, it will lead. It will no doubt provide more convincing and carefully worked out explanations for the use of a medium of exchange than we now have, but it is probable that those explanations will not be fundamentally different from the traditional verbal explanations. Furthermore it is doubtful that this work will have any major consequences for the way macromodels are built [Fischer, 1975, p. 159].

This evaluation is misleading. Technically, for example, Madden [1976] has shown that the Ostroy–Starr process requires some traders to engage in utility decreasing trade. Consequently any monetary bilateral trade sequence that goes to equilibrium involves speculation in the sense that some agents at time t accept something they don't want in the hope that it can be exchanged at time $t+1$ for something they do want. The Keynesian concern with time and uncertainty makes a reappearance in precisely the context Keynes stressed, a monetary economy. Further, this view provides a monetary theory context to support Clower's view of the notional–effective demand split since workers can be thought of as speculators in monetary markets for labor services.

The major monetary theoretic point is brought out clearly by Weber who is led to *define* money as "the generally accepted means of current payment or promised future payment for a group or society . . . the primary determinant of whether or not a good becomes a medium of exchange is the prior probability which traders assign to its being acceptable for a later trade" [Weber, 1977, p. 11].

This definition resembles Clower's [1971, 1976] except that Clower requires payment in organized markets. The Edgeworthian system, however, shows that this is irrelevant in the definition of money. The stress on organized markets is a neo-Walrasian atavism. It is more appropriate to suggest that the extensive demand for means-of-payment money in these exchange processes will *lead* to the creation of organized markets. In a practical sense, these ideas feed immediately into macromodels by the way in which the "supply of money" is defined. Current discussion of the M_1–M_5 definitions are not unrelated to these microfoundations problems.

At a more profound level it must recognized that monetary theory has never been well integrated with sophisticated models of systemic coordination. As noted earlier, in their *General Competitive Analysis*, Arrow and Hahn quote Keynes' statement that "the importance of money essentially flows from its being a link between the present and future." They go on to "add that it is important also because it is a link between the past and the present. If a serious monetary theory comes to be written, the fact that contracts are indeed made in terms of money will be of considerable importance" [p. 357].

Even if this is a bit overstated, it is clear that Edgeworthian disequilibrium analysis qualifies as "serious monetary theory" since the role of money, at least in the Ostroy–Starr, Clower, and Weber type of analysis, is specific to the means by which exchange contracts may be arranged and debts discharged. A government which requires "money" to settle tax liabilities is not irrelevant to the story.

Part III

"What ought to be done is neglected,
What ought not to be done is done."

The Dhammapada

10

A brief conclusion

In Chapter 1, we suggested that the end result of the study of the microfoundations of macroeconomics would look different to different kinds of economists. The objectives of a microeconomist might be met by presenting a reasonably detailed structure in which various well-understood market failures would lie at the heart of macroeconomic conundrums like inflation and unemployment. To a macroeconomist, a successful reconciliation of micro and macro might entail a return to Marshallian price theory, or a well worked out statement of individual behavior in a non-optimizing framework. To a historian of thought, it would be a reasonable sort of endeavor if it could explain how the neo-Walrasian and Keynesian research programs grew, grew apart, and what features of each made them appear incompatible.

After our efforts in Part II, however, matters become somewhat clearer. Stripping the idea of general equlibrium theory down to models of interrelated and systemic interaction, there is almost an embarrassment of riches in the sense that it is no longer the case that a general equilibrium framework itself determines uniquely the kind of macroeconomics one can do. Gone are the days when general equilibrium theory required only numeraire money, no production, fulfilled expectations, Walras' Law, tatonnement price adjustments, reversible time, futures markets for all commodities, an equilibrium defined by market clearing, etc. To argue that

157

general equilibrium theory provides no theory of unemployment because the theory assumes Walras' Law may have been a useful way to indulge oneself in the late 1930s, but it is irrelevant to general equilibrium theory today.

In Chapter 5, we examined the coordination success–coordination failure method of distinguishing microeconomics from macroeconomics. The primary value of this perspective was that it allowed an integrated microfoundations vision to be identified; we subsequently examined some recent studies as examples of interactive systems which carried within them the potentiality for both order and chaos, both harmony and inefficiency.

General equilibrium theory, in the sense of the work of the past twenty years surveyed in Part II, encompasses these various concerns. One can only talk of equilibrium in the context of outcomes of equilibration processes, and equilibration itself needs the reference point of some distinguishable outcome to give form to the interactive process. Consequently, any analysis which could even potentially serve as a piece of the microfoundations of macroeconomics story will involve a general equilibrium theoretic perspective.[1]

Grant that the questions micro theorists and macro theorists wish to ask and answer with this system may differ. Grant that these differences may ramify into even different private languages. Further grant that A's language may imply that B's question is not well posed. Even granted all these facts, without a general model of systemic interaction capable of producing both coordination success and coordination failure neither microeconomics nor macroeconomics will be more than theory fragments, partial explanations of limited scope and content.

Varieties of general equilibrium theory

How well do the modes of general equilibrium theorizing described in Part II accord with the evaluative criteria based on

---

[1] Perhaps catastrophe theory can provide such a perspective. See O'Shea, 1976; Peixoto, 1973; Poston and Stewart, 1976; Smale, 1966; Thom, 1975, 1976; Zeeman, 1968, 1973. But also see Kolata, 1977.

general systemic interactions? It certainly is a fair criticism that Walrasian equilibrium, Walrasian disequilibrium, Edgeworthian equilibrium and Edgeworthian disequilibrium are imperfect categories. An analysis of temporary equilibrium with quantity rationing fits into the first two pigeonholes, while recontracting with money could conceivably fit in all but the first box. What should be recognized, however, is that within each category the models do bear a family resemblance. Various models within a category are elaborations and generalizations of others within the category. That is not to say that there exists a canonical Walrasian disequilibrium model, say, but rather that all such models share some features like disequilibrium trading in a market environment.

The basic lesson of Part II is thus not that one or the other of the categories has produced a model of *the* microfoundations of macroeconomics but rather that looking for such a single model is a foolish way to do any science, even economics. The age of the great system builders has passed, not because of a lack of genius today to rival Walras or Keynes, but rather because economics has progressed beyond what Kuhn once called the "pre-paradigm" stage of development as a science. The research programs of modern economic theory, based on the neo-Walrasian synthesis developed many years ago, have transcended their simple beginnings to constitute on-going activity involving the elaboration of approaches to problem solving.

Economic theory, of the sort we have been examining, has a useful history in the phrasing and answering of questions: Why doesn't the price of oil fall; what will be the effect of credit card banking; how many jobs will a tax reduction create? The neo-Walrasian synthesis, as it has developed, provides a context for such enquiries. At the same time the negative heuristic for the program rules out as impermissible certain other questions. "Does alienation increase when mechanization occurs?" is regarded as a non-question for modern economic theory.

Despite these positive accomplishments, general equilibrium theory must be wary of claiming too much. There is not now any model which successfully integrates micro and macro theory. That economists desire such a model reflects the level of methodological discourse in our discipline. The large number of models surveyed, for example, in Chapter 7 all serve to suggest ways, on occasion mutually inconsistent ways, in which disequilibrium adjustment structures the manner in which models can be constructed. As a result, how one chooses to "fit" money into a disequilibrium process is limited only by what linkages one wishes to have to other partial theories of a monetary economy. One would use a different approach to modelling, even with a general equilibrium system, if one were interested in inflation rather than macro problems of branch banking. Economic knowledge is constructed piece by piece, using partial explanations which are better fitted into the nooks and crannies of our discipline than other partial explanations. Models are metaphors, explaining one structure in terms of another. If the actual economy is that which we seek ultimately to understand, simplified models are indispensable since only the economy is a perfect model of itself. Barring logical error, the value of a model depends on the purposes of its use by the economist whose understanding of the economy is always in terms of those metaphors most congenial to his mind.

A final world

What is now called for, in evaluating the microfoundations literature, is tolerance on the part of economists of all persuasions.

That general equilibrium theory should guide the insights that we have about economic processes is, at first glance, a rather surprising fact of life. Its explanation goes deeper than assertions about Walras' influence, the demise of Marshallian and English economics, and the growing professional influence of economists who believe in the hypothetico-deductive mode of inquiry based on the construction of mathematical models.

What I am suggesting, of course, is that there is something "natural" about general systems theory. Identifying mathematical or similarly abstract reasoning with general equilibrium theory does that theory an injustice. As Thom has remarked [1975, p. 5]:

"I am certain that the human mind would not be fully satisfied with a universe [economy] in which all phenomena were governed by a mathematical process that was coherent but totally abstract."

It is well to note that economists too have been continually suspicious of exaggerated claims about abstract tools. Nobel Laureate Tjalling Koopmans, no enemy of formal reasoning, once cautioned in his famous *Three Essays* that:

> it should perhaps be said that the success of a mathematical tool or theory in one field (such as physics) creates no presumption either for or against its usefulness in another field (such as economics). But each transfer of a tool between fields is attended by a risk . . . The test of suitability of a tool of reasoning is whether it gives the most logical and economical expression to the basic assumptions appropriate to the field in question, and to the reasoning that establishes their implications . . . The difficulty in economic dynamics has been that the tools have suggested the assumptions rather than the other way around [1957, pp. 182–3].

The preceding pages have suggested that the question of appropriate microeconomic foundations for macroeconomic theory is still an open one. General equilibrium analysis, has, for a number of years now, gone far beyond Walrasian typologies to a consideration of many issues, like transactions structures, information costs, speculation, imperfect adjustment, and search behavior, which are nearer to traditional macroeconomic concerns. There should be little argument about the proposition that some sort of revivified, reconstituted general equilibrium theory is the only logically possible general link between microeconomics and macroeconomics. Those who argue that the analysis at present prejudges the issue fail to appreciate the variety of modern general equilibrium theory. Those who argue that the current theory is unrealistic fail to appreciate the attention being paid to real adjustment processes in real time. And yet the subject, being so current, is not susceptible to neat packages of integrated results. Although one may guess that eclecticism will be the rule in the near future, it is apparent that many issues are being faced. If answers are emerging only slowly, it is because the problems are difficult and not because general equilibrium theorists have failed to ask hard questions.

BIBLIOGRAPHY

Allingham, Michael. *Equilibrium and Disequilibrium.* Cambridge, Mass.: Ballinger Press, 1973.

Arrow, Kenneth J. "The Organization of Economic Activity" in *The Analysis and Evaluation of Public Expenditure Compendium on PPBS, Volume 1.* Joint Economic Committee Print. 91st Congress, 1st session. Washington: U.S.G.P.O., 1969.

Arrow, Kenneth J., Block, H. D. and Hurwicz, Leo. "On the Stability of the Competitive Equilibrium, Part II," *Econometrica,* Jan. 1959, 27(1), pp. 82–109.

Arrow, Kenneth J., and Debreu, Gerard. "Existence of an Equilibrium for a Competitive Economy," *Econometrica,* July 1954, 22(3), pp. 265–90.

Arrow, Kenneth J., and Enthoven, Alain C. "A Theorem on Expectations and Stability of Equilibrium," *Econometrica,* July 1956, 24(3), pp. 288–93.

Arrow, Kenneth J., and Hahn, Frank H. *General Competitive Analysis.* San Francisco: Holden Day, 1971.

Arrow, Kenneth J., and Hurwicz, Leo. "On the stability of the Competitive Equilibrium, Part I," *Econometrica,* Oct. 1958, 26, pp. 522–52.

Arrow, Kenneth J., and Nerlove, Marc. "A Note on Expectation and Stability," *Econometrica,* April 1958, 26, pp. 297–305.

Aumann, Robert, J. "Markets with a Continuum of Traders," *Econometrica,* Jan.–Apr. 1964, 32, pp. 39–50.

Baligh, Helmy, Graham, Daniel A., Weintraub, E. Roy, and Weisfeld, Morris. "Real Transactions Costs Are Inessential," *Kylos,* 29(3), 1976, pp. 527–31.

Barro, Robert J. "A Theory of Monopolistic Price Adjustment," *Review of Economic Studies,* Jan. 1972, 39(1), pp. 17–26.

Barro, Robert J. and Grossman, Herschel I. "A General Disequilibrium Model of Income and Employment," *American Economic Review,* March 1971, 61(1), pp. 82–93.

Baumol, William J. and Goldfeld, Stephen [eds.]. *Precursors in Mathematical Economics,* LSE Series of Scarce Works on Political Economy, number 19. London: London School of Economics, 1968.

Benassy, Jean-Pascal. "Neo-Keynesian Disequilibrium Theory in a Monetary Economy," *Review of Economic Studies*, Oct. 1975, 42(4), pp. 503–23.

– "Theorie du Desequilibre et Fondements Microeconomiques de la Macroeconomie," Paris, CEPREMAP paper no. 7505, July 1975, mimeo.

Boehm, Volker "The Core of an Economy with Production," *Review of Economic Studies*, July 1974, 41(3), pp. 429–36.

Boehm, Volker, and Lévine, P. "Temporary Equilibrium with Quantity Rationing," CORE Discussion Papers, no. 7614, Louvain, Belgium, 1976.

Cassel, Gustav. *Theory of the Social Economy.* New York: Harcourt Brace, rev. ed., 1932.

Champseur, P., Dreze, J. and Henry, C. "Dynamic Processes in Economic Theory," CORE Discussion papers no. 7417, Louvain, Belgium, 1974.

Clower, Robert W. "The Keynesian Counterrevolution: A theoretical Appraisal," in [Hahn and Brechling, 1965] and in [Clower, 1970], pp. 270–97.

– "A Reconsideration of the Microfoundations of Monetary Theory," *Western Economic Journal*, Dec. 1967, 6(1), in [Clower, 1970] pp. 202–12.

– [ed.] *Monetary Theory.* Baltimore: Penguin Books, 1970.

– "The Anatomy of Monetary Theory," UCLA, Department of Economics Working Paper # 79, August 1976, mimeo.

Coddington, Alan, "Varieties of Keynesianism," *Thames Papers in Political Economy.* London: Thames Polytechnic, 1976.

Cournot, Augustin. *Researches into the Mathematical Principles of the Theory of Wealth*, trans. N. Bacon, Homewood, Illinois: Irwin, facsimile of 1838 edition, paperback, 1963.

Davidson, Paul. *Money and the Real World.* New York: Wiley, Halsted Press, 1972.

– "Why Money Matters: A Postscript," Rutgers Economics Discussion Paper, 1977, mimeo.

– "Money and General Equilibrium," *Economie Appliqueé*, 1977.

Davidson, Paul, and Smolensky, Eugene. *Aggregate Supply and Demand Analysis.* New York: Harper and Row, 1962.

Debreu, Gerard. *The Theory of Value.* New York: Wiley, 1959.

Debreu, Gerard and Scarf, Herbert. "A Limit Theorem on the Core of an Economy," *International Economic Review,* Sept. 1963, 4, pp. 235–46.

De Jong, F. J. "Supply Functions in Keynesian Economics," *Economic Journal,* March 1954, 64(253), pp. 3–24.

Diamond, Peter A. "A Model of Price Adjustment," *Journal of Economic Theory,* June 1971, 3(2), pp. 156–68.

Dixit, Avinash. "Public Finance in a Keynesian Temporary Equilibrium," *Journal of Economic Theory,* 1976, 12, pp. 242–58.

Dorfman, Robert, Samuelson, Paul A. and Solow, Robert M. *Linear Programming and Economic Analysis.* New York: McGraw Hill, 1958.

Drèze, Jacques H., ed. *Allocations Under Uncertainty, Equilibrium, and Optimality.* London: Macmillan, 1973.

– "Existence of an Exchange Equilibrium Under Price Rigidities," *International Economic Review,* June 1975, 16(2), pp. 301–20.

Edgeworth, Francis Y. *Mathematical Psychics.* London: Routledge, 1881.

Eichner, Alfred. *The Megacorp and Oligopoly*. New York: Cambridge University Press, 1974.

Feldman, Allan M. "Bilateral Trading Processes, Pairwise Optimality, and Pareto Optimality," *Review of Economic Studies,* Oct. 1973, 40(4).

– "The Stability of a Random Paretian Reallocative Process," Brown University Discussion Paper, Providence, R.I., 1973.

– "Recontracting Stability," *Econometrica,* Jan. 1974, 42(1), pp. 35–44.

Fischer, Stanley. "Recent Developments in Monetary Theory," *American Economic Review*, May 1975, 65(2), pp. 157–66.

Fisher, Franklin M. "Quasi-Competitive Price Adjustment by Individual Firms: A Preliminary Paper," *Journal of Economic Theory,* June 1970, 2(2), pp. 195–206.

– "On Price Adjustment Without an Auctioneer," *Review of Economic Studies,* Jan. 1972, 39(1), pp. 1–16.

– "Stability and Competitive Equilibrium in Two Models of Search and Individual Price Adjustment," *Journal of Economic Theory,* Oct. 1973, 6(5), pp. 446–70.

– "The Stability of General Equilibrium: Results and Problems" in Michael Artis and Robert Nobay [eds.] *Essays in Economic Analysis.* Cambridge: Cambridge University Press, 1976, pp. 3–29.

Gale, D. "The Law of Supply and Demand," *Mathematica Scandinavica,* 1955, 37 pp. 155–69.

Graham, Daniel A., Jacobson, Edward and Weintraub, E. R. "Transactions Costs an the Convergence of a 'Trade out of Equilibrium' Adjustment Process," *International Economic Review,* Feb. 1972, 13(1), pp. 123–31.

Graham, Daniel A., Peterson, D., Jennergren, P. and Weintraub, E. R. "Trader-Commodity Parity Theorems," *Journal of Economic Theory,* June 1976, 12(3), pp. 443–54.

Graham, Daniel A., and Weintraub, E. R. "On Convergence to Pareto Allocations," *Review of Economic Studies,* July 1975, 42(3), pp. 469–72.

Grandmont, Jean M. "On the Short Run Equilibrium in a Monetary Economy," in Drèze, J. [1973], 1971.

– "Temporary General Equilibrium Theory," *Econometrica,* April 1977, 45(3), pp. 535–72.

Grandmont, Jean M. and Laroque, Guy. "Money in a Pure Consumption Loan Model," *Journal of Economic Theory,* August 1973, 6(4), pp. 382–95.

– "On Money and Banking," *Review of Economic Studies,* 42, 1975, pp. 207–36.

– "On Temporary Keynesian Equilibria," *Review of Economic Studies,* Feb. 1976a, 43(133), pp. 53–7. In [Harcourt, 1977].

– "On the Liquidity Trap," *Econometrica,* 44, 1976b, pp. 129–35.

– and Younes, Yves. "Disequilibrium Allocations and Recontracting," Stanford (IMSSS) Discussion Paper #186, mimeo, 1976.

Grandmont, Jean M. and Younes, Yves. "On the Role of Money and the Existence of a Monetary Equilibrium," *Review of Economic Studies,* July 1972, 39(3), pp. 355–72.

– "On the Efficiency of Monetary Equilibrium," *Review of Economic Studies,* April 1973, 40(2), pp. 149–66.

Green, Jerry R. "Temporary General Equilibrium in a Sequential Trading Model with Spot and Future Transactions," *Econometrica,* Nov. 1973, 41(6), pp. 1103–24.

– "The Stability of Edgeworth's Recontracting Process," *Econometrica*, Jan. 1974, 42(1), pp. 21–34.

Green, H. A. John. "Aggregation Problems of Macroeconomics," 1977, in [Harcourt, 1977].

Grossman, Herschel I. "Theories of Markets Without Recontracting," *Journal of Economic Theory,* Dec. 1969, 1(4), pp. 476–9.

Haavelmo, Trygve. *A Study in the Theory of Investment.* Chicago, 1960.

Hahn, Frank H. "Gross Substitutes and the Dynamic Stability of General Equilibrium," *Econometrica,* 1958, 26, pp. 169–70.

– "On Some Problems of Proving the Existence of an Equilibrium in a Monetary Economy," in Hahn, F. H. and Brechling, F. 52 [1965], 1965.

– "Some Adjustment Problems," *Econometrica,* Jan. 1970, 38(1), pp. 1–17.

– "Equilibrium with Transactions Costs," *Econometrica*, May 1971, 39(3), pp. 417–39.

– *On th Notion of Equilibrium in Economics.* Cambridge: Cambridge University Press, 1973.

– "On Transaction Costs, Inessential Sequence Economies and Money," *Review of Economic Studies*, Oct. 1973, 40(4), pp. 449–62.

– "Keynesian Economics and General Equilibrium Theory: Reflections on Some Current Debates," 1977, in [Harcourt, 1977].

Hahn, Frank H. and Brechling, F. P. R. *The Theory of Interest Rates.* London: Macmillan, 1965.

Hahn, Frank H. and Negishi, Takashi. "A Theorem on Non-Tatonnement Stability," *Econometrica*, July 1962, 30(3), pp. 463–69.

Hansen, Bent. *A Survey of General Equilibrium Systems.* New York: McGraw-Hill, 1970.

Harcourt, Geoffrey C. [ed.] *The Microeconomic Foundations of Macroeconomics,* Proceedings of a Conference held by the IEA at S'Agara, Spain in April, 1975, London: Macmillan, 1977.

Harrod, Roy F. *The Life of John Maynard Keynes.* New York: St. Martins Press, 1966, rev. ed.

Hart, O. D. "On the Existence of Equilibrium in a Securities Model," *Journal of Economic Theory,* Sept. 1974, 9(3), pp. 293–311.

Hey, J. D. "Price Adjustment in an Atomistic Market," *Journal of Economic Theory,* Dec. 1974, 8(4), pp. 483–99.

Hicks, John R. *Value and Capital.* Oxford: Oxford University Press, 1939.

– *The Crisis in Keynesian Economics.* New York: Basic Books, 1974.

Hildenbrand, Werner. "Existence of Equilibria for Economies with Production and a Measure Space of Consumers," *Econometrica*, Sept. 1970, 38(5), pp. 608–23.

Hines, Albert G. *On the Reappraisal of Keynesian Economics.* London: Martin Robertson, 1971.

Hurwicz, Leo. "The Design of Mechanisms for Resource Allocation, *American Economic Review,* May 1973, 63(2), pp. 1–30.

Hurwicz, Leo, Radner, Roy and Reiter, Stanley. "A Stochastic Decentralized

Resource Allocation Process, Parts I and II," *Econometrica*, March 1975, 43(2), pp. 187–221; 43(3), pp. 363–94.

Intrilligator, Michael D. and Kendrick, David A. [eds.] *Frontiers of Quantitative Economics, Volume II.* New York: American Elsevier, 1974.

Iwai, Katsuhito. "The Firm in Uncertain Markets and Its Price, Wage, and Employment Adjustments," *Review of Economic Studies*, April 1974, 41(2), pp. 257–76.

Kakutani, Shizuo, "A Generalization of Brouwer's Fixed Point Theorem," *Duke Mathematical Journal*, 1941, 8, pp. 457–9.

Kaldor, Nicholas. "The Irrelevance of Equilibrium Economics," *Economic Journal*, Dec. 1972, 82(328), pp. 1237–55.

Keynes, John Maynard. *The General Theory of Employment, Interest, and Money.* New York: Harcourt Brace, 1936.

– *The Collected Writings, Volume VIII: The Treatise on Probability*, edited by Donald Moggridge, London: Macmillan, 1973.

– *The Collected Writings, Volume XIII: The General Theory and After: Part 1 – Preparation*, edited by Donald Moggridge, London: Macmillan, 1973.

– *The Collected Writings, Volume XIV: The Genral Theory and After: Part II – Defence and Development*, edited by Donald Moggridge, London: Macmillan, 1973.

Klein, Lawrence R. *The Keynesian Revolution*, 2nd ed., New York: Macmillan, 1966.

Kolata, Gina Bari. "Catastrophe Theory: The Emperor Has No Clothes," *Science*, 196, April 1977, p. 287 and pp. 350–1.

Koopmans, Tjalling. *Three Essays on the State of Economic Science.* New York: McGraw Hill, 1957.

Kornai, Janos. *Anti-Equilibrium.* New York: American Elsevier, 1971.

Kregel, J. A. "Economic Methodology in the Fact of Uncertainty," *Economic Journal*, June 1976, 86(342), pp. 209–25.

Kurz, Mordecai. "Equilibrium in a Finite Sequence of Markets with Transaction Cost," *Econometrica*, Jan. 1974, 42(1), pp. 1–20.

Lakatos, Imre. "Falsification and the Methodology of Scientific Research Programmes" in [Lakatos and Musgrave, 1970].

Lakatos, Imres and Musgrave, Alan [eds.] *Criticism and the Growth of Knowledge.* Cambridge: Cambridge University Press, 1970.

Lange, Oscar. *Price Flexibility and Employment.* Bloomington: Principia Press, 1944.

Latsis, Spiro. [ed.] *Method and Appraisal in Economics.* Cambridge: Cambridge University Press, 1976.

Leijonhufvud, Axel. "Keynes and the Keynesians: A suggested Interpretation," *American Economic Review*, 57(2), 1966 in [Clower, 1970, pp. 298–310].

– *On Keynesian Economics and the Economics of Keynes.* New York: Oxford University Press, 1968.

– *Keynes and the Classics.* London: Institute of Economic Affairs, 1969.

– "Effective Demand Failures," *Swedish Journal of Economics*, March 1973, 75(1), pp. 27–58.

– "Varieties of Price Theory: What Microfoundations for Macrotheory?" UCLA

Discussion Paper, Los Angeles, 1974.

- "Schools, 'revolutions', and research programmes in economic theory" in [Latsis, 1976], pp. 65–108.

Liapunov, A. "Probleme general de la stabilite du movement," *Annales de Toulouse*, 1907, 9. p. 2.

Madden, Paul J. "Efficient Sequences of Non-Monetary Exchange," *Review of Economic Studies*, Oct. 1975, 42(4), pp. 581–96.

- "A Theorem on Decentralized Exchange," *Econometrica*, July 1976, pp. 787–92.

McKenzie, Lionel W. "On the Existence of General Equilibrium for a Competitive Market," *Econometrica*, Jan. 1959, 27(1), pp. 54–71.

- "Stability of Equilibrium and the Value of Positive Excess Demand," *Econometrica*, July 1960, 28(3), pp. 606–17.

- "The Matrix with a Dominant Diagonal and Economic Theory," in *Mathematical Methods in Social Sciences*. Edited by K. Arrow, L. Karlin and P. Suppes. Palo Alto: Standford University Press, 1960.

- "Market Equilibrium and Uncertainty: Comment" in [Intrilligator, 1974].

Metzler, Lloyd A. "Stability of Multiple Markets: The Hicks Conditions," *Econometrica*, 13, (1945), pp. 277–92.

Minsky, Hyman P. *John Maynard Keynes*. New York: Columbia University Press, 1975.

Negishi, Takashi. "A Note on the Stability of an Economy Where All Goods are Gross Substitute," *Econometrica*, July 1958, 25, pp. 445–7.

- "On the Successive Barter Process," *Econ. Stud. Quart.*, 1962, 12, pp. 61–4.

- "The Stability of a Competitive Economy: A Survey Article," *Econometrica*, Oct. 1962, 30(4), pp. 635–69.

Nikaido, Hakukane. *Convex Structures and Economic Theory*. New York: Academic Press, 1969.

O'Shea, D. "An Exposition of Catastrophe Theory, and Its Applications to Phase Transitions," *Papers in Pure and Applied Mathematics, number 47*. Kingston, Ontario: Queen's University, 1976, mimeo.

Ostroy, Joseph M. "The Informational Efficiency of Monetary Exchange," *American Economic Review*, Sept. 1973, 63(4), pp. 597–610.

Ostroy, Joseph M. and Starr, Ross M. "Money and the Decentralization of Exchange," *Econometrica*, Nov. 1974, 42(6), pp. 1093–1114.

Patinkin, Don, "Price Flexibility and full Employment," *American Economic Review*, Sept. 1948, 38(4), pp. 543–64; as corrected in *Studies in Monetary Economics*. New York: Harper and Row, 1972.

- *Money, Interest, and Prices*. Second edition. New York: Harper and Row, 1965.

- "Keynes' Monetary Thought: A Study of its Development," *History of Political Economy*, Spring 1976, 8(1), pp. 1–150.

Peixoto, M. M. "On the Classification of Flows on 2-Manifolds" in Peixoto, M. M. [ed.] *Dynamical Systems*. New York: Academic Press, 1973.

Phelps, E. S., ed. *Microeconomic Foundations of Employment and Inflation Theory*. New York: Norton, 1970.

Poston, Tim and Stewart, Ian. *Taylor Expansions and Catastrophes*. Research Notes in Mathematics, number 7, London: Pitman, 1976.

Rader, Trout. "Pairwise Optimality and Non-Competitive Behavior," in *Papers in Quantitative Economics.* Edited by J. Quirk and A. M. Zarley. Lawrence: University of Kansas Press, 1968, pp. 101–27.

Radner, Roy. "Competitive Equilibrium Under Uncertainty," *Econometrica,* Jan. 1968, 36(1), pp. 31–58.

– "Problems in the Theory of Markets Under Uncertainty," *American Economic Review,* May 1970, 60(2), pp. 454–60.

– "Market Equilibrium and Uncertainty: Concepts and Problems" in [Intrilligator, 1974].

Rapoport, Anatol. *Fights, Games and Debates.* Ann Arbor: University of Michigan Press, 1960.

Riker, William H. and Ordeshook, Peter C. *An Introduction to Positive Political Theory.* Englewood Cliffs: Prentice Hall, 1973.

Roberts, David. *Keynes and the System of the Keynesians,* unpublished Ph.D. dissertation, Duke Univeristy, 1975.

Robinson, Joan. *Economic Heresies.* London: Macmillan, 1971.

Rothschild, Michael. "Models of Market Organization with Imperfect Information: A Survey," *Journal of Political Economy,* Nov./Dec. 1973, 81(6), pp. 1283–1308.

Sagan, Carl. *The Dragons of Eden.* New York: Random House, 1977.

Samuelson, Paul A. *Foundations of Economic Analysis.* Cambridge: Harvard University Press, 1947.

– "The Monopolistic Competition Revolution," in *Monopolistic Competition Theory: Studies in Impact.* Edited by R. Kuenne. New York: Wiley, 1967.

Scarf, Herbert. "Some Examples of Global Instability of the Competitive Equilibrium," *International Economic Review,* Sept. 1960, 1. pp. 157–72.

Shackle, G. L. S. *Epistemics and Economics.* Cambridge: Cambridge University Press, 1972.

– *Keynesian Kaleidics.* Edinburgh: Edinburgh University Press, 1974.

Shubik, Martin. "Edgeworth Market Games," in *Contributions to the Theory of Games.* Vol IV. Edited by A. W. Tucker and R. O. Luce. Princeton: Princeton University Press, 1959.

– "The General Equilibrium Model is Incomplete and Not Adequate for the Reconciliation of Micro and Macroeconomic Theory," *Kyklos,* 1975, 28(3), pp. 545–73.

– *A Theory of Money and Financial Institutions,* unpublished. Chapters as Cowles Foundation Discussion papers, Yale University, 1970–1977.

Sondermann, Dieter. "Temporary Competitive Equilibrium Under Uncertainty," in Drèze [1973].

– "Economies of Scale and Equilibria in Coalition Production Economies," *Journal of Economic Theory,* Sept. 1974, 8(3), pp. 259–91.

Smale, Stephen. "Structurally Stable Systems are not Dense," *American Journal of Mathematics,* 88, 1966, pp. 491–6.

Smithies, Arthur. "The Stability of Competitive Equilibrium," *Econometrica,* 10, 1942, pp. 258–74.

Starrett, David. "Inefficiency and the Demand for 'Money' in a sequence Economy," *Review of Economic Studies,* Oct. 1973, 40(4), pp. 437–48.

Stigum, Bernt P. "Competitive Equilibrium Under Uncertainty," *Quarterly Journal of Economics,* November 1969.
– "Market Equilibrium and Uncertainty: Comment" in [Intrilligator, 1974].
Takayama, Akira. *Mathematical Economics.* Hinsdale, Illinois: The Dryden Press, 1974.
Thom, René. *Structural Stability and Morphogenesis,* trans. by D. H. Fowler. Reading, Mass.: W. A. Benjamin, Inc., 1975.
– "The Two-Fold Way of Catastrophe Theory" in P. Hilton [ed.] *Structural Stability, The Theory of Catastrophes, and Applications in the Sciences.* Lecture Notes in Mathematics, Volume 525. New York: Springer-Verlag, 1976.
Uzawa, Hirofumi. "On The Stability of Edgeworth's Barter Process," *International Economic Review,* 3, May 1962.
Von Bertalanffy, Ludwig. "Comments on Professor Piaget's Paper" in Tanner, J. M. and Inhelder, Bärbel [eds.] *Discussions on Child Development, Volume IV.* London: Tavistock Publications, 1960.
Von Neumann, John. "Über ein Ökonomishes Gleichungs-System und eine Verallgemeinerung des Browershen Fixpunktsatzes" in Menger, Karl [ed.] *Ergebnisse eines Mathematischen Killoquiums,* 8, 1935–1936, Vienna, 1937, trans. by G. Morton as "A Model of General Economic Equilibrium," *Review of Economic Studies,* 13, 1945–1946, pp. 1–9.
Wald, Abraham. "Über einige Gleichungssysteme der mathematishe Ökonomie," *Zeitschrift fur Nationalökonomie,* 7, 1936, pp. 637–70, trans. as "On Some Systems of Equations in Mathematical Economics," *Econometrica,* 19, Oct. 1951, pp. 368–403.
Walsh, Vivian Charles. *Introductory to Contemporary Microeconomics.* New York: McGraw Hill, 1970.
Weber, Warren, "What is Money, Anyway?" Duke University Economics Department, mimeo, 1977.
Weintraub, E. R. *General Equilibrium Theory.* London: Macmillan, 1974.
– *Conflict and Cooperation in Economics.* London: Macmillan, 1975a.
– "Uncertainty and the Keynesian Revolution," *History of Political Economy,* December, 1975b.
– "Creating the Neo-Walrasian Synthesis," *Economie Appliqueé,* 1977.
Weintraub, Sidney. "The Microfoundations of Aggregate Demand and Supply," *Economic Journal,* March 1957, 67(265), pp. 455–70.
– *An Approach to the Theory of Income Distribution.* Philadelphia: Chilton, 1958.
Wells, Paul. "Keynes' Aggregate Supply Function: A suggested Interpretation," *Economic Journal,* March 1960, 70(277), pp. 536–42.
– "Keynes' Employment Function," *History of Political Economy,* 1974, 6(2), pp. 158–62.
Wigner, Eugene P. "The Unreasonable Effectiveness of Mathematics in the Natural Sciences" in Thomas L. Saaty and F. Joachim Weyl [eds.], *The Spirit and The Uses of The Mathematical Sciences.* New York: McGraw Hill, 1969, pp. 123–140.
Wilson, E. O. *Sociobiology.* Cambridge, Mass.: Harvard University Press, Belknap Press, 1975.
Wilson, Robert. "The Game Theoretic Structure of Arrow's General Possibility

Theorem," *Journal of Economic Theory,* August 1972, 5(1), pp. 14–20.

Zeeman, E. Christopher. "Lecture Notes on Dynamical Systems." Mathematisk Institut, Aarhus Universitat, 1968, no pagination, mimeo.

– "Applications of Catastrophe Theory," *International Conference on Manifolds: Proceedings.* Tokyo: Tokyo University, 1973, pp. 11–23.

INDEX OF NAMES

SUBJECT INDEX

174